Published by:

Dan Norder, Inklings Press
226 E. Oklahoma Ave.
Knoxville, TN 37917 USA

www.inklings.com

ISBN-13: 978-0-9789112-9-4
ISBN-10: 0-9789112-9-6

The Victims of
Jack the Ripper

Neal Stubbings Shelden

- *Inklings Press* -

CONTENTS

INTRODUCTION

Oh no, not another Jack the Ripper book! Full of blood and gore and making ridiculous claims about famous Victorian artists, actors or doctors! Will it also reveal another diary allegedly written by the killer in 1888 or more than likely in the 1970's?

So who was Jack the Ripper then?

Well, I don't know and in this book you will not find out, it does not contain the solution to the crimes. Neither will it take a look at the main suspects, or reflect on what the government or the senior and subordinate police officers believed at the time. For expert views on all of those subjects I thoroughly recommend you read the books by Evans, Sugden, Rumbelow, Begg et al.

In this book, I concentrate solely on the victims of Jack the Ripper who can be listed as Mary Ann Nichols, Annie Chapman, Elizabeth Stride, Catherine Eddowes and Mary Jane Kelly. Many authors and researchers consider there to be more victims than the canonical five, for instance Martha Tabram found murdered on the 7th August 1888. Other murders before Nichols and after Kelly could have been by the same hand, but there was no proof for them to be included. In 1986, I started out on my research quest believing there was only five victims, and twenty one years later I still hold that point of view.

In the last few years, I have made some great new finds with my own family tree that connect me directly to the places where the victims of Jack the Ripper once lived. On my father's side, I have Joseph Russell Piddington, who ran the Sir John Barleycorn public house at 18 Upper North Street at exactly the same time that John and Elizabeth Stride ran the coffee house opposite. Little did I know back in 1986 when I found the Strides in the 1870 post office directory that my own great great great grandfather was living in the same street. Elizabeth Stride was later buried in the East London Cemetery where my ancestor had been buried six years previous.

On the subject of husband John Stride, my great great grandfather

Josiah Gaster followed the same route from living at Poplar High Street to the Poplar and Stepney Sick Asylum where he also died but at a much later date. His inquest on the 23rd February 1916 was conducted by Wynne E. Baxter, Coroner for three of the inquests of the Ripper victims.

My great grandfather, Charles Stubbings, was a true Eastender and was born in 1869 a short walk from Hanbury Street at Albert Cottages. Another connection with Hanbury Street goes back to my Huguenot ancestors, the Bouvier family. In 1826, my great great great grandfather Samuel Bouvier lived at Brown's Lane in Spitalfields that eventually became a part of Hanbury Street. At the same time his father lived at 14 Wood Street (today Wilkes Street), a weaver's house still standing today round the back of the Ten Bells public house and now worth many millions. The Bouvier families also had many children baptized at Shoreditch Church, Spitalfields Church, and in the 1770's lived in Brick Lane.

William Barrett, the brother-in-law of my great grandmother Jane Norton went to World War One as a private in the 2nd Battalion of the South Wales Borderers. He was killed in 1915, and his name was included on the Helles Memorial at Gallipoli in Turkey. On the same memorial is the name of Eric Nichols, grandson of Mary Ann Nichols, who died one month later.

On my mother's side, the Rowe family lived and worked in the Wapping area and could have passed by Mary Jane Kelly plying her trade in the Pennington Street or St George's Street area in the 1880's.

My great great grandmother's brother Edward Cole was serving as a fireman at Shadwell Fire Station in 1888 and could have been called on to fight the large fire that raged down at the docks on the night Mary Ann Nichols was murdered.

To top all of that, was the most surprising revelation in my family history that I discovered no more than one year ago and concerned my missing great great grandmother Eliza Cole. I was initially searching for her daughter (my great grandmother) Alice Cole and finally tracked her down in the records of Dr Barnardo's Children's Home at Barkingside.

Alice had been born in Maldon Workhouse in Essex when her mother Eliza was aged only 17. Afterwards, Eliza abandoned her child and Alice went to live with her grandmother. In about 1880, Eliza

Cole found her way to Brentwood in Essex and lived in at least two addresses there, at Weald Lane she paid a rent of 2s 6d per week. In about October 1886, Alice was sent by her grandmother to live with Eliza in Brentwood due to the grandmother's poverty.

So what is the significance of all this I hear the reader cry?

Well, in the highly detailed Barnardo's records, my great great grandmother Eliza Cole was described as being spoken of as a most degraded prostitute! The record also states that Eliza was better known by the appellations of Fat Eliza and Black Eliza. She was with a young man who appeared to be living off her prostitution, and it was alleged she ill-treated her daughter by making her drunk several times. There was also another child, a boy, who had a different father to Alice.

Alice was eventually rescued by an unnamed lady in Brentwood and sent to an orphanage in Upper Clapton in London, before being admitted to Barnardo's on the 22nd March 1888.

I cannot be certain what happened to Eliza Cole after March 1888, but her son was placed in the Billericay Workhouse by the time of the 1891 census. My guess is that she packed up her stuff and finally left Brentwood, and was just as likely to have ended up in London as anywhere else in Essex, maybe to join with her contemporary street walker sisters Nichols, Chapman, Stride, Eddowes and Kelly.

The fact that after twenty one years of research into the victims of Jack the Ripper I have now found a Catherine Eddowes in my own family, I am beginning to believe in the word fate!

During my years as a Ripperologist I have many people to thank for their interest and assistance, and none more so than the descendants of the victims. In particular, the great granddaughter of Annie Chapman for her continued permission to use the Annie Chapman photograph, and her mother for the same. To Maureen Adamson for her enthusiasm and support for the cause, and for taking time to research avenues of her family history beyond my reach. To the granddaughter of Alice Esther Nichols for permission to use the photograph donated. To Josephine and Jan, for sparing the time for film crews, DNA tests, and other reasons, always generously willing to help. To Jean the daughter of Ellen Mary Ann Wells the same. To the son of Violet Wells, and to Susan the daughter of Catherine Wells for the interest shown in their ancestor. Also, to Tracey and mother Jean Smith, for all their kind endeavours to help me with the great new finds on the Thomas Phillips family line, and to all Phillips descendants. Thanks to Mrs Stevenson, a descendant of Charles William Fisher, for his photograph too.

I am indebted to Dan Norder for the publication of this book without whom it would simply not have happened. Dan contacted me in 2006 with an offer to publish any future works, and one year on from that first approach he has generously lent his time in difficult circumstances to get this book into print.

My thanks to Andy Aliffe and to all the team of the Jack the Ripper 2007 UK Conference. To have my name added to the list of the recipients of the Outstanding Achievement Award is a recognition highly appreciated and unexpected.

A big thank you too to Mike James at True Detective Magazine, and The Jack the Ripper A-Z team Paul Begg, Martin Fido and Keith Skinner for the initial recognition that got the ball rolling many years ago, and to everyone involved with Ripper Notes, The Ripperologist, Ripperana, and the Casebook: Jack the Ripper Internet Site, especially Stephen P. Ryder, for their continued interest in the victim's research.

For their kind words of encouragement over the years, Christopher-Michael DiGrazia, Stewart Evans, Robert McLaughlin, Donald Rumbelow, and Thomas Schachner to name but a few, and to Loretta Lay and Richard Dixon Smith for helping to sell my previous publications. Sorry to anyone who might have been inadvertently omitted, my humble thanks go to one all.

Hopefully, one day a memorial to the victims of Jack the Ripper will be unveiled in Spitalfields or the City of London, but until then we can only wait and hope!

Neal Stubbings Shelden 2007.

MARY ANN NICHOLS

She was born Mary Ann Walker on Tuesday 26th August 1845 at Dawes Court, Shoe Lane in the City of London. The daughter of Edward Walker, a locksmith, and his wife Caroline (née Webb). The parents was married on 17th February 1840 at St Mary's Church in Lambeth, while they both lived at Oakley Street. Caroline Webb was the daughter of a sawyer Edmund Webb, and the groom was the son of John Walker a carman.

Edward and Caroline's first child was born south of the river in 1843 and named after his father. After Mary, a third child was born in about 1849 and named Frederick. By the 1851 census the family lived at 14 Dean Street, a lodging house off Fetter Lane in the City. Caroline Walker worked as a laundress, while her daughter probably attended school during the subsequent years.

By 1861, Caroline and Frederick were dead and Edward and his remaining two children lived at 19 Harp Alley in the City of London. Her father Edward Walker had become a blacksmith by 1864. To date, it has not been possible to know why Caroline died, as a death certificate cannot be found, but it's not unlikely that Frederick might of caught a contagious illness from her which cost him his life too – or even the other way round?

Finally, a happy event happened in the family when Mary married on Saturday 16th January 1864 at the nearby St Bride's Church in Fleet Street. The groom was William Nichols a printer from Oxford born in about 1842 and the son of a herald painter of the same name. Banns were called on the 27th December, the 3rd and 10th January, and the witnesses was provided for the service by the parish. William Nichols once worked as a warehouseman and lived previously at 30-31 Bouverie Street.

In 1865 or 1866, a son was born to the couple at Camberwell and named Edward John Nichols. A second son Percy George was born on the 18th July 1868 at 131 Trafalgar Street, Walworth Road in St Saviour.

A year later, William and Mary were witnesses at the marriage of her brother Edward Walker, an engineer, to Mary Anne Ward on Christmas Day 1869 at St Peter's Church in Walworth.

On the 1871 census, Mary's new baby a 7 month old daughter named Alice Esther, and her widowed father was living at their house. The old blacksmith eventually went to live with his son and his family at Guilford Street, Walworth.

Five years later William and his wife became one of the first tenants in the newly built (1875) Peabody Buildings in Duchy Street, Stamford Street Estate. They moved into Tenement No.3, Block D, on the 31st July 1876. It had four rooms at a rent of 6s 8d per week, rates 1s 7d. Nichols was recorded as working for 30s per week as a printer for William Clowes and Sons, type music and general printers of Duke Street. At the same time, a widow from Hampshire and her three children lived next door at No.5, Block D. Her name was Sarah Vidler and she had a daughter by a previous marriage named Rosetta Walls. Rosetta worked as a charwoman and was born at Marylebone in about 1853-1854.

Edward Walker made the claim in 1888 that Nichols had carried on an affair with the woman that nursed his daughter whilst she was having their fourth child. The child Eliza Sarah Nichols was born in December 1876 and the birth registration reveals that Mary was living away from William at No.3, Block J. However, in the archives of the Peabody Estates, the tenant at that address appears to be the widow of a Harrison, who lived there with her son. Although, it's not out of the question that Harrison was having an affair with Nichols, it seems less likely when we consider that Harrison was 20 years older than Rosetta Walls. With the wife away at another tenement block, no doubt Nichols turned his attention to the young woman living next door. By 1st February 1877, Mary returned home to him.

On 4th June 1877, the couple and their four children moved on to the cheaper No.6, Block D. There was only three rooms, and the rent was 5s per week, rates 1s 2d. Their last son Henry Alfred was born there a year later on the 4th December 1878. We can presume that William continued to meet with Rosetta despite the reconciliation with his wife, because the final separation came just over a year later. Mary left home during Easter 1880 and left the children behind with their father. Her addiction to alcohol and his apparent infidelity were reasons given for the separation. Their eldest son Edward John also left in about 1881 to live with his grandfather Edward Walker.

William left Peabody Buildings on the 28th July 1882, where the record remarks, left in debt, otherwise good tenant. The next year, Rosetta gave birth to William's child in Camberwell and called him Arthur Nichols Walls. But it would not be until 1894 that the couple finally married in the same area, six years after the murder of his wife.

Mary was admitted to Lambeth Workhouse at Renfrew Road during 1882 and 1883, and she resumed some level of respectability by living with her father and afterwards with a man named Thomas Stuart Drew. Drew was a blacksmith of York Mews, 15 York Street in Walworth, and was a widower from early 1884 when his wife Matilda died leaving him the single parent of their three children. Mary, three years younger, moved in with him sometime between 1884 and her return to life in the workhouse in October 1887.

The last time her father saw her alive was at the funeral of his eldest son Edward Walker that took place on Saturday 5th June 1886 at the Camberwell Old Cemetery in Forest Hill Road. Father and daughter was not on speaking terms at the time due to some bad feeling between them which had resulted in her leaving his home three or four years earlier.

Full details about the untimely death of her brother Edward Walker was reported in the South London Chronicle on the 5th June 1886, under the heading of ANOTHER PARAFFIN LAMP FATALITY. The inquest was held on the 3rd June by the Deputy Coroner for the district Sam F. Langham. (In 1888, as Coroner for the City of London he conducted the Catherine Eddowes inquest).

In 1886, Mary's brother, Edward Walker and his wife lived at 52 Coleman Road, Southampton Street in Camberwell. On the night of Monday 31st May, the couple sat talking in the kitchen for half an hour until it was around midnight. When Mrs Walker left the room to go to bed there was suddenly a loud explosion, she turned and saw that her husband's hair was alight when he attempted to put out a paraffin lamp. The mantelpiece was ablaze. Mrs Walker immediately screamed for the assistance of their lodger John Barton, who at once rushed downstairs and put out the fire. Walker was hurriedly taken in a cab to Guy's Hospital where he was admitted suffering from severe burns to the right side of his face and chest. He died at 7.15 p.m. on the 1st June. The inquest verdict was accidental death.

Mary was now the last of the Walker children still alive, but her life was destined to be equally as short. On the 25th October 1887, she entered St Giles Workhouse in Endell Street. The next day she left for Edmonton Workhouse, and at a later date she returned to Lambeth Workhouse where she spent her last Christmas.

She then went on to Mitcham Workhouse where an order of removal sent her back to Renfrew Road on the 16th April 1888. Reported in the Camberwell and Peckham Times for the 8th September, was that in response to her good conduct at Lambeth Workhouse, the matron Mrs Fielder, procured employment for her at a house in Wandsworth and she left to commence with the new opportunity she had been given on the 12th May 1888.

She wrote to her father from there:

I just write to say you will be glad to know that I am settled in my new place and going all right up to now. My people went out yesterday and have not returned so I am left in charge. It is a grand place inside with trees and gardens back and front. All has been newly done up. They are teetotallers and very religious so I ought to get on. They are very nice people and I have not much to do. I do hope you are all right and the boy has work. So goodbye now for the present. Yours Truly Polly. Answer soon please and let me know how you are.

Walker returned a letter to his daughter, but on the 14th July, a postcard was received at the workhouse from her mistress Mrs Sarah Cowdry intimating that Nichols had absconded taking with her goods to the value of £3 10s. From then on, Mary Ann Nichols, nicknamed Polly, wandered around the streets and public houses where she met with fellow workhouse inmate 30 year old Mary Ann Monk.

Edward John Nichols, the eldest son and an engineer, lived with his grandfather at 16 Maydwell Street in Camberwell. William Nichols, who had not seen his wife for three years, and his eldest son for about six or seven years, worked for a firm of letter press printers called Perkins, Bacon and son., of Whitefriars Street in the City of London. Son Percy George followed his father's occupation.

Unbeknown to her family and friends, Mary crossed the river and settled herself in amongst the East End community. There she spent a day to day existence of earning pennies as a prostitute to pay for her insatiable lust for the bottle, and a bed for the night at a Spitalfields common lodging house. It is difficult to know how long she had lived the life of a streetwalker, but it could be assumed that she began in the early 1880's when her father and husband were aware that she was regularly in the company of other men.

At 2.30 a.m., on Friday 31st August 1888, Mary met a former fellow lodger of 18 Thrawl Street, at the corner of Osborn Street and Brick Lane. Ellen Holland tried to persuade her to return to the lodging house after Nichols boasted that she had spent the money for her doss that night on drink. Nichols refused and went off to walk the streets once more in the Whitechapel Road in the hope of finding the money to return to her doss at 56 Flower and Dean Street.

At about 3.40 a.m., a carman named Charles Cross was passing through Buck's Row in Whitechapel, on his way to work when he discovered a dead body of a woman lying by a stable yard gate. Another man, Robert Paul, was close behind Cross and the two men hurried away to find a policeman.

Meanwhile, P.C. John Neill, 97J walked along his usual beat and also came across the body, he summoned the assistance of another constable. Within a quarter of an hour, Dr Rees Llewellyn arrived and pronounced life extinct. Her throat had been severely cut with a moderately sharp long-bladed knife. A full examination at the mortuary of the Workhouse Infirmary in Old Montague Street revealed the horrific extent of the abdominal wounds. The inquest was conducted by Coroner Wynne E. Baxter on the 1st, 3rd, 17th, 22nd September.

Edward Walker, William Nichols and Edward John Nichols, all went to see her body lying in the mortuary and on the 6th September attended her burial in a public grave at the City of London Cemetery in Ilford.

Mary Ann Nichols was 43. She was described as 5ft 2ins tall, with dark brown hair turning grey, brown eyes, a dark complexion, two teeth missing, a good figure, and a small childhood scar on her forehead that her husband said was made larger years before her death when she was knocked down by a cab in Lambeth and taken to St Thomas' Hospital. She always kept herself very clean and tidy, and her character was described as good-tempered.

Two months after the completion of his mother's inquest, Edward John Nichols married Lillian Mary Oxley on the 27th November 1888 at Emmanuel Church, Camberwell. He was then living at 34 Clarendon Street. On the 1891 census the couple again lived with grandfather

Edward Walker and by that time had a son named Edward Wilfrid Nichols born in 1890. They had another son Arthur Nichols in 1895 while living at Waterloo Road, but he died shortly afterwards. Edward Walker either left Maydwell Street in 1898, or might have died?

By the 1901 census, William and Rosetta had two more children together, Ethel M. and Winifred C. Nichols. Arthur had followed his father and half brother Henry Alfred as a machine printer.

Son Edward John Nichols was living with his wife and four children at 1 Upton Villa, Upton Road, Bexley in Kent. The last child Eric Nichols was born across the River Thames at Plaistow in Essex. Edward John was a foreman mechanical engineer. He died aged about 42-43 on the 15th September 1908 at the Edmonton Workhouse. His occupation was recorded by then as a tool maker journeyman, and his address was 99 South Street, Ponders End, Enfield. He died of a carcinoma of the sub maxillary gland, and exhaustion, and was buried at Enfield Highway Cemetery. His widow Lilian Mary married twice more before she died aged 75 in 1942 and was buried at Herne Bay in Kent.

The children of Edward John and Lilian Mary have now been thoroughly researched. Eldest son, Edward Wilfrid Nichols, a family favourite known to some as Uncle Tont, emigrated to Canada and lived in Strathcona in Manitoba. In 1914, he joined the Canadian Overseas Expeditionary Force, and served in the 2nd Canadian Contingent Mounted Rifles. On his Attestation Paper he was described as 5ft 7ins tall, with a fair complexion, blue eyes, fair hair, and his occupation was given as a machinist. The Medical examination considered him to be fit. After the First World War, he married Ethel who had two daughters of her own. Edward Wilfrid then worked for a railroad in Manitoba, and was killed in 1947 when a door fell off a boxcar. He was buried on the 20th June at Transcona Cemetery.

Edward John and Lilian's eldest daughter, Florence Elizabeth Nichols remained in England. She married Thomas Clarence Tate, and had six children, two boys and four girls. The two youngest Tate daughters eventually went to live in Canada, but two other children died when young. Their son, Herbert George Tate died aged 23 whilst serving in the Royal Navy on board HMS Marigold during World War Two. On the 9th December 1942, he was a leading stoker when the warship was torpedoed and sunk by Italian aircraft off the coast of Algiers. Herbert George Tate was named among his comrades on the Chatham Naval Memorial. His mother Florence Elizabeth died in the 1960's.

The third child of Edward John and Lilian to reach adulthood was Lilian Nichols. She followed her eldest brother and moved to Canada in 1914, where she married twice and made British Columbia her home. With Peter Macdonald, she had three children, the eldest in 1919 was named Lilian Ethel Macdonald and two boys followed. Lilian Ethel married William Cassidy and had five children, one of which is Maureen Adamson who is now a grandmother herself. Lilian died in 1969, and Lilian Ethel died in 2004.

Eric Nichols, Edward John and Lilian's youngest child, became a private in the Royal Marine Light Infantry, Deal Bn R.N., during World War One. He died aged only 17 on the 26th June 1915, and is named on the Helles Memorial that stands on the tip of the Gallipoli Peninsula in Turkey.

Mary Ann Nichols' second eldest son, Percy George Nichols, married his first wife Ada Amelia Crombleholme on the 1st July 1899 at St Giles Church in Camberwell. They lived at Camberwell Green and were unlikely to have had any children. Ada's death in 1926 was reported in the Islington Gazette as Barnsbury Woman's Sudden Death, with the cause of death being a rupture of the left coronary artery. Percy remarried in 1936 at the Islington Register Office to Elizabeth Gell, but in 1948 a similar story about how he had died aged 80 was reported in The Islington Gazette on Friday 22nd October under the heading HOLLOWAY ROAD MISHAP - INQUEST ON AGED MAN. Percy George was struck by a van but survived for two months until he died at home from a ruptured aneurysm. The inquest verdict was accidental death.

Alice Esther Nichols was married to a letter sorter William Samuel Edwards on the 26th June 1897 at St George's Church in Camberwell. They had two daughters, and the photograph of her and her family was kindly provided by her granddaughter.

Eliza Sarah Nichols, remains the only line yet to be traced, but does not appear to have been with her father William Nichols when he died on the 14th July 1917 at 13 Kelmore Grove in Camberwell. He died aged 77 of valvular disease of the heart. His second wife Rosetta was the informant. Eliza Sarah had lived with her sister back in 1901 but then seems to disappear from the records?

Lastly, Henry Alfred Nichols, a printer, married Ada Alice

Quarterman in 1910 at Dulwich and lived at Ashbourne Grove. His father William had retired by then. The couple very likely remained childless and lived in the Camberwell area all their lives. Henry Alfred was a retired printers machine manager by the time he died aged 88 on the 13th November 1967 at the Wilkinson Home in Peckham. He died ten years after his wife, and the cause of death was recorded as bronchopneumonia, chronic bronchitis.

ANNIE CHAPMAN

It seemed that little more could be added to the history of Annie Chapman until Ripper writer and researcher Chris Scott came across a fascinating newspaper article in a Canadian newspaper the Manitoba Daily Free Press for the 9th January 1892. This article appeared to be a longer version than others that appeared in 1889 in the Pall Mall Gazette and newspapers in the USA.

The story concerned a letter clearly written by Annie's sister Mirium Ruth Smith as a concerned member of the local congregation of the Rev. John MacNeill, and in it she gives a warning of the dangers of unfermented wine and the way in which it had damaged the lives of her parents, her sister and brother. I believe these articles to be too accurate not to be true, and therefore include details taken from them to reconstruct the previously known life and history of Annie Chapman.

Annie was born to George Smith and Ruth Chapman in about September 1840-1841?

George Smith was born the son of a shoemaker Thomas Smith and his wife Ann (née Staples), on the 12th April 1819, at Waddington in Lincolnshire. For a time he followed his father's trade until he went to London to enlist in the 2nd Regiment of Life Guards on 11th December 1834. Ruth Chapman was born about 1818 the daughter of William and Isabella Chapman at Herstmonceaux, Sussex. Her father was also a shoemaker and they lived at 101 Gardiners Street.

Annie Eliza Smith, her full maiden name, was probably born at least six to eighteen months prior to her parents wedding on the 22nd February 1842. The ceremony took place at St James Church, Paddington. George Smith gave his address as Harrow Road, while his bride lived at Market Street.

Their second daughter Emily Latitia Smith (named after aunt Latitia Smith) was born at 4 Rutland Terrace, Knightsbridge, and was christened a month later on the 8th December 1844 at Holy Trinity

Church, Brompton. The family had moved by then to 3 Montpelier Place, Knightsbridge. It was later claimed by her aforementioned sister that Annie started drinking when she was quite young, and that they was the children of intemperate parents.

Two more children were born at the parish of Clewer in Windsor, Berkshire. Georgina on 1st April 1856 at 12 Keppel Terrace, and two years later Mirium Ruth on 27th October 1858. The frequent changes in residence were directly the result of George Smith's military service that required annual manoeuvres from one barracks to another, including Hyde Park-Kensington, Upper Albany Street-Regents Park and Windsor. We can assume that all the children received a good standard of education, or at least that Annie's education was likely to have been superior to the other Ripper victims.

During another short period in London at 6 Middle Row North in Knightsbridge, their last child Fountain Hamilton Smith was born on 25th February 1861. They then returned to Clewer at 7 Keppel Terrace, where they appeared on the 1861 census. Annie had already left home by then to gain work, and was probably Annie Smith aged 21 a servant living with another servant 62 year old Mary Ford at 2 Duke Street, off Oxford Street in Westminster.

George Smith's discharge certificate from the Life Guards described him as 6ft tall, with brown eyes and hair, and a fair complexion. His character was excellent and he was awarded a pension of 1s 1½d per day. He was never promoted beyond the rank of private, but received four distinguishing marks for good conduct on the 9th July 1860. In the course of twenty-five years service he would have attended some of the most important events of the time, such as Queen Victoria's marriage to Prince Albert in 1840, and the funeral of the Duke of Wellington in 1852. He retired at his own request just prior to his 43rd birthday at Horse Guards in London.

When he left military service he became a valet, but died in circumstances clouded in mystery in about 1864. According to Mirium Ruth's letter their father took his own life by cutting his throat. She blamed alcohol for his suicide, but until a death certificate can be discovered the real reason for why he killed himself must remain speculative at best. Whatever happened to George, his widow did indeed take the family back to Knightsbridge where her name was first recorded as a resident on the poor rate book at 29 Montpelier Place.

On Saturday 1st May 1869, Annie Eliza Smith was married to a coachman named John Chapman at All Saints Church, Ennismore Gardens in Knightsbridge. John was the son of George Chapman and was born in 1844 at Newmarket, and was unlikely to be related to Annie's mother of the same surname. Annie's sister Emily Latitia attended as a witness with George White, a gentleman's coachman, and friend of John's. White lived with his wife at 1 Brooks Mews North in Bayswater, and John and Annie went to live there after the wedding. In 1870, a Mrs Ponsford was paying the rates for the property and owned the stable.

Annie returned to her mother's house to give birth to her first child Emily Ruth Chapman on 25th June 1870, and they were again staying at Montpelier Place by the time of the 1871 census. Then on the 5th June 1873, Annie gave birth to a second daughter Annie Georgina Chapman. By then John worked for a nobleman at Bond Street, so the family moved to nearby 17 South Bruton Mews, Berkeley Square in Mayfair. She was christened on 27th June at All Saints Church, and given an additional middle name of Jane which was never used on subsequent occasions. (Only Annie Georgina herself mistakenly wrote her middle name as Jane on a copy of her marriage certificate before crossing it out to write in Georgina).

Prior to 1880, the family moved again to start a new life in Clewer in Berkshire, where John, Annie and the children lived in the apartments over the stables on the land of the St Leonards Hill Mansion. John had found work as a coachman and domestic servant for Sir Francis Tress Barry who was apparently a man well known in the area for his philanthropy. (Barry bought St. Leonard's Hill in 1872 and rebuilt the original house, he became a baronet in 1899 and M.P. for Windsor from 1890 to 1906). Both of the Chapman daughters attended school, one in particular (probably Annie Georgina) was educated at a highly respectable ladies school in Windsor with the cost of her tuition being defrayed by one of Annie's sisters. However, the eldest daughter Emily Ruth began to suffer from epileptic fits from 1878.

On the 21st November 1880, Annie gave birth to a boy and called him John Alfred Chapman whilst staying at Water Oakley in Bray a short distance from Windsor. The boy was a cripple and his mother took him to London for a time to place him in a hospital. Annie's sister later blamed her excessive drinking for his condition, and also claimed that she had given birth to eight children in all, with the ones that failed to live also being victims of the alcoholic curse. There is every possible reason to believe that Annie could have had five still-born babies because the percentage rate of stillborns in Victorian England was very high, but with such a slim chance of a child's survival in those days through all kinds of causes, a child who was born to an alcoholic would be very unlikely to live.

During the 1881 census, Annie and her three living children were visiting her mother at Knightsbridge and that was possibly when she sought medical help for the boy?

John Chapman's brother Alfred, was living with his wife and daughter Emily at 14 Lincoln's Inn Fields in St Giles. He worked as an office keeper at a solicitor's office, and could have received several visits by John and his family.

Also in 1881, we can find Emily Latitia Smith living at 128 Walton Street in Chelsea, today Harrods is close by, but back then even Knightsbridge and Chelsea had a working class population. Emily was a dressmaker, and sister Mirium Ruth also a dressmaker was with her on the census record. Mirium had become a religious convert in about 1875 and her sisters apart from Annie followed suit. The Halkin Street Church was one of the places where they worshipped, and Mirium, Emily and Georgina all signed an abstinence pledge two years later and tried to persuade Annie to do the same. She did so, but kept resorting back to the bottle. At one time she went into what was called a home for the cure of the intemperate, and John paid 12p per week for her to stay there

One year later, and apparently a sober and changed woman Annie returned to a normal life for a few months and this could be when she went back with her children to Berkshire, but she was still unwelcome at the farm cottage. It might be a fairy tale, but her drinking habits seemingly returned when she kissed her husband as he was off to work after drinking a glass of hot whisky for his cold symptoms, Annie then went out and in less than an hour was back to her old self as the drunken mad woman.

On the 26th November 1882, her eldest daughter Emily Ruth died of meningitis after suffering for five days. She was only 12 years old. Caroline Aylesbury, probably the children's nanny witnessed the child's death, and although her father could have been working away from home, Annie is likely to have been present. Mirium again, later blamed Annie's alcoholism for Emily's death, but meningitis is a common killer even today and has nothing to do with the mother's taste for whisky or rum. We can only imagine the grief and devastation both parents felt for their loss, and in 1884 their broken lives were about to go through further irreversible changes. The Windsor and Eton Gazette for the 15th September 1888 reported that her dissolute habits made it imperatively necessary that she should reside elsewhere than on the gentleman's grounds. John reluctantly obliged to separate from his wife and this set in motion a tragic sequence of events for himself and his family.

Annie Chapman, well known throughout the neighbourhood of Clewer and Windsor was often seen wandering about the country like a common tramp. After living for a short time in Windsor she left for London and the hovels of Spitalfields. Annie was already on bad terms with her mother and sister Georgina and stayed so right up until her own death. No doubt, they strongly disapproved of her lifestyle in the East End where she became a familiar face and at times resorted to prostitution on the Spitalfields streets. She could be the same Annie Chapman charged at the Thames Magistrates Court in October 1885 with a stealing a hammer. This evidence might also confirm as true the reason that John left his job in Bond Street in the 1870's was because he was fired due to his wife's dishonesty?

During mid-1885, John Chapman sent a family bible to his daughter, and in a hand that was unlikely to be his was written the words, Annie Georgeina Chapman, A Birthday Present from her Loving Father, June 5th 1885.

Fountain Hamilton Smith married on the 14th February 1886 to Edith Annie Lunn at the same church his eldest sister was married All Saints Church in Knightsbridge. He was a stationer and lived at his mother's house paying a rent of 6s per week for a furnished ground floor room.

In the summer of that year, John Chapman described by his sister-in-law as a white haired, broken hearted man, resigned his job at the cottage in Clewer because of ill health and went to stay at Grove Road in New Windsor. As his sickness began to take hold of him, the 10s per week he sent to his wife payable to her at Commercial Road suddenly stopped, and a tramp-like woman called at The Merry Wives of Windsor public house in Spital Road, Clewer. Annie had walked all the way from London and slept overnight at a lodging house in Colnbrook. She had been told of her husband's illness, maybe by her brother-in-the-law who lived at Oxford Street in Whitechapel, and walked across town to find out whether it was true or merely an excuse for him not to send money. She wanted to know where he was living, but it is unlikely they met at Grove Road.

The landlord saw her leave the public house shortly afterwards and she was never seen in the area again. When she returned to Whitechapel she began a relationship with a man named Edward Stanley.

John Chapman died aged 42 on Christmas day 1886 at 1 Richmond Villas, Grove Road in New Windsor, after suffering for six months with cirrhosis of the liver-ascites, and dropsy. He was receiving charity before he died and elderly friend Sally Westell from the almshouses in Victoria Street was present.

Annie Georgina Chapman might have lived with her father at Grove Road until he died, but was also reported to have spent time in a boarding school or possibly the ladies school already mentioned. Farcical stories in 1888 that she was sent to a French Institution, or became a member of a circus performing troupe are dismissed entirely as a myth by her family.

Her brother John Alfred Chapman was allegedly placed in a charitable school outside Windsor where his mother would occasionally visit him. Annie also visited one of her sister's at Vauxhaull in South London and received 5d and her family would also give her clothes and tried to discourage her from her lifestyle, but her alcohol addiction meant that in her own words, she must and would have the drink.

In Spitalfields she was nicknamed Dark Annie Sievey because she once lived with a sieve maker in Dorset Street nicknamed Jack Sievey. When she died on the morning of Saturday 8 September 1888, her doss was at Crossingham's lodging house, 35 Dorset Street.

Timothy Donovan, deputy, and John Evans, night-watchman, both spoke with Annie when she was in the lodging house at about 1.35 a.m. She appeared to be the worse for drink, but clearly felt ill, and also had bruising to her chest from a fight during that week with a fellow lodger named Eliza Cooper. Evans watched as she left at about 2.00 a.m. and headed in the direction of Brushfield Street, after appealing to him to see that Donovan did not let her bed.

A woman named Elizabeth Long walked along Hanbury Street at about 5.30 a.m. and saw a woman she later identified as Chapman talking to a man on the pavement outside number 29. Long overheard the man say, Will you? To which the woman replied, Yes. Long described a jewish looking man, a little taller than 5ft, aged around 40, with a dark complexion, shabby-genteel appearance, and wearing a deerstalker hat and dark coat.

Albert Cadosch, who lived at 27 Hanbury Street, was in the backyard when he heard a voice from the yard next door say, No! It was followed soon after by something falling against the partition fence. He thought nothing of it and went off to work.

John Davis, who lodged with his family at 29 Hanbury Street, got up from bed and walked down to the backyard just before 6.00 a.m. There he found a woman lying on the floor between the steps and the fence with her throat cut and body terribly mutilated. Davis rushed out into Hanbury Street and attracted the assistance of workmen Henry John Holland, James Kent, and James Green, who after taking a look at the body ran back out of the house again and in various directions. Davis towards the local police station.

When the police arrived in the form of Inspector Joseph Chandler, he took charge of the crime scene and sent for Dr George Bagster Phillips who arrived at 6.30 a.m. At the post mortem, Phillips discovered that her womb had been removed. Her friend in Spitalfields, Amelia Palmer, identified her body later that day.

Coroner Wynne E. Baxter presided over the inquest on 10th, 12th, 13th, 19th and 26th September which ran concurrently with the Mary Ann Nichols case.

Annie was described as 5ft tall, with blue eyes, a large prominent nose, a fair complexion, and dark brown wavy hair. She was stout and well proportioned, with two teeth deficient in her lower jaw. She was clever and industrious and would go to Stratford East to sell crochet work (antimacassars) and baskets she made or to sell flowers in the street. A very respectable, quiet, but sociable woman, who never used bad language, was well educated and often read in her leisure time. When she died aged 47 or 48, she was already dying from disease of the lungs and brain.

Her brother Fountain had also identified her body, and on the 12th September the burial took place at Manor Park Cemetery and was attended and paid for by the family.

Only a month later, Fountain caused further heartache for the family when he was sacked for drinking and thieving from his job as a manager of a warehouse in the city. Afterwards, friends of his got him a job in Oxford Street but again after only a month he took to drink and absconded with some money, leaving his wife and two children penniless. Eventually, he surrendered himself to police in Gloucester and was brought back to London and tried at Marlborough Street Court, he blamed the drink. He was sentenced to three months hard labour at Millbank Prison, and his sister Mirium was later refused entry to see him.

Emily Latitia Smith finally married a widower William Cox on the 24th December 1888 at Woodstock Register Office in Oxfordshire. Emily was older than her husband and called her father George Smith a deceased house steward on the register. William Cox was a blacksmith and lived at Moor Street in Kidlington, and the couple were there together on the 1891 census with four of William's children. Also living there was Annie Georgina Chapman, Annie's 17 year old daughter. This confirms the original belief that Emily Latitia took a responsible interest in the future of her niece as she became a young woman. According to family tradition, Annie Georgina once worked as a servant to a court dressmaker before she was married. Taking Mirium's words into consideration, it's very likely that Annie Georgina and her brother and even their aged grandmother Ruth was not informed of the tragedies to hit the family.

By the time of the census of 1891, Annie's son John Alfred Chapman was back living with his family at 29 Montpelier Place, his aunt and probably his guardian Georgina Smith gave her occupation as a laundress. Ruth Smith died aged 75 in 1893, and her daughter Georgina became owner-occupier of the house. In 1901, John Alfred was recorded on the census as being paralysed from infancy. Fountain Hamilton Smith had four children one named George was born in the USA in about 1891-1892, but by 1901 the family was back living in England at 6 Reporton Road in Fulham. His son Howard Hamilton Smith married Ellen Maud Taylor on 10th September 1910 at St Clements Church, Fulham. He was an engineer and lived at 7 Bothwell Street.

The two spinster sisters Georgina and Mirium Ruth Smith remained at Montpelier Place until 1927, then moved on to 17 Radnor Walk in Chelsea.

Emily Latitia Cox died aged 86 of chronic bronchitis on the 12th February 1931 at Hensington within, Woodstock. Her stepson Richard Cox was the informant.

Fountain died on 24th October 1933 aged 74 at the Radcliffe Infirmary, Oxford. The cause of death was acute intestinal obstruction (strangled inguinal hernia). He was a retired house decorator and lived at 26 London Road, Chipping Norton.

On 4th January 1940, Mirium Ruth died aged 81 of cerebral thrombosis at St Luke's Hospital. Georgina, who would have been greatly affected by her sister's passing died aged 84 of a haemorrhage from a chronic gastric ulcer, over a month later on 13th February.

ELIZABETH STRIDE

She was born Elizabeth Gustafdotter on 27th November 1843 in the parish of Torslanda in Sweden. She was one of four children, with two brothers Carl and Svante and an older sister Anna Christina belonging to Gustaf Ericsson, a small farm owner and his wife Beata Carlsdotter. She went to the local parish school. Her mother died in 1864, and her sister married a shoemaker Bernard Olsson in Gothenburg. Elizabeth had worked as a domestic servant in Gothenburg since 1860, but in 1865 she was registered as a prostitute in the Gothenburg police files. She also gave birth to a stillborn girl one month later. (Klas Lithner article about Elizabeth Stride's Swedish history in True Detective Magazine, December 1987 edition).

In 1866, she travelled to England and London's East End where on 10th July she was registered at the Swedish Church, Princes Square, St George's-in-the-East. In common with many Swedish women who came to England at that time, she shortened her surname to Gustifson, and found work as a domestic servant to a gentleman's family living in the West End.

On Sunday 7th March 1869, she married at the parish church of St Giles-in-the-Fields to John Thomas Stride, a carpenter of 21 Munster Street, Regents Park. The bride was staying at a lodging house 67 Gower Street run by a 64 year old widow named Elizabeth Bond.

John Thomas Stride, was almost twice her age, and was born in about 1821 the son of a shipwright William Stride, and his wife Eleanor (née Monk) at Sheerness in Kent. The family were Wesleyan Methodists. Elizabeth invented a name for her father of Augustus Gustifson on the marriage register, quite possibly with the prior consent of the groom because his own brother's name was Frederick Augustus Stride. The witnesses at the wedding were W. Taylor, sexton of the church, and Daniel Fryatt, who was recorded in post office directories as a coffee room proprietor of 6 Munster Street.

Soon afterwards, Stride himself opened a coffee hall in the East

End at Upper North Street, Poplar. In 1871, they moved to another coffee hall at 178 Poplar High Street, and staying there with them when the census was taken was a visitor aged 15 from Portsmouth named Charles Thew.

Elizabeth's father-in-law, William Stride, died on the 6th September 1873 at 3 Stride's Row, Mile Town, Sheerness, in Kent. In his will he left No 4 Tenement in Stride's Row to his son Edward Stride to be put in his possession six months after his decease. To his daughter Sarah Ann Snook and her children the same terms for No 7 and 8 Tenement. Daniel Elisha Stride was left No's 1, 2, 3, 5, 6, Tenements and the overall responsibility for Stride's Row. Also, a stable, plots of ground, a coal shed, a workshop, and two tenements at Victory Street. William's effects of under £600 was proved at the Principal Registry by his son Daniel Elisha Stride and nephew Charles Stride. John Thomas Stride didn't receive a penny, so we cannot know as to whether he and Elizabeth were invited to the funeral? Some of the money had perhaps inspired the ambitions of one of the Stride family because on the Sheerness 1901 census Daniel Stride, the son of Daniel Elisha, was calling himself a writer.

During 1874-1875, John Thomas Stride and Elizabeth lived three doors along from their previous address at 172 Poplar High Street, perhaps a lodging house for foreign seamen. Mr North, who was likely to have been the publican Francis North of The Blakeneys Head opposite at 143 Poplar High Street, knew both Elizabeth Stride and her husband and saw her daily until 1879 and thereafter less frequently. (In 1888, Police Constable Daniels came forward with North to identify her body, according to a report in The Illustrated Police News for the 27th October 1888).

On the 21st March 1877, a police constable took her to Poplar Workhouse where it was written down that she had been brought from the Thames Magistrates Court, at Arbour Square in Stepney.

On the 3rd September 1878, the paddle-steamer the Princess Alice sank after a collision with a collier on the River Thames at Galleons Reach and at least 600 people perished. According to North, Elizabeth Stride once told him that she was trying to get some money from the Mansion House Fund set up to give aid to the victims families. He did not believe her claims that her husband was one of the victims, but she continued to tell the story right throughout her life.

Her father Gustaf Ericsson died in 1879 in Sweden and she may well have been informed of his death? Elizabeth created a fantasy world for herself, which suggests that she was continuously attempting to escape her past, and therefore might never have heard from family after leaving Sweden?

On the 1881 census, Elizabeth and her husband were living at 69 Usher Road, Old Ford Road in Bow. She later claimed to her friends in Spitalfields that she had many children, some in school and others with friends of her husband, but it was almost certainly untrue. Whatever the truth was behind her story telling, they separated that year and her alcoholism was one of the causes.

She was admitted on the morning of Wednesday 28th December 1881 to Whitechapel Workhouse Infirmary at Bakers Row, suffering from bronchitis and was sent Ward A2. She gave her address as Brick Lane, where she lived for the past fortnight.

Elizabeth left the infirmary on 4th January 1882 and entered Whitechapel Workhouse at South Grove for three days and was then discharged. Subsequently, she found lodgings at 32 Flower and Dean Street in Spitalfields, and often returned there up until the time of her death.

In 1884, John Thomas Stride was admitted to the Poplar Union Workhouse for one day in August. He was then sent on to the Poplar and Stepney Sick Asylum at Devons Road in Bromley, where he died aged 63 of heart disease. He was buried in a public grave at the City of London Cemetery on 30th October. Again, how, and when, Elizabeth heard about his death cannot be ascertained, or equally how his death affected her, but she continued to tell associates that he had died on the Princess Alice.

Only a few weeks later on 13th November, the newly widowed Elizabeth appeared again at Thames Magistrates Court, charged with being drunk and disorderly, and soliciting prostitution. She was sentenced to seven days hard labour. Her most familiar beats to ply her trade in London's East End was at Commercial Road East to as far afield as Stratford and Bow.

In 1885, she became acquainted with Michael Kidney, an Irish dock labourer, and lived with him intermittently at Devonshire Street, Commercial Road. They had a largely ambivalent relationship, because Kidney strongly objected to her going on the streets and her heavy drinking bouts, and at times he probably resorted to violence. In January 1887, Elizabeth made a complaint of assault against him, and after a short stay on 24 March at St George's-in-the-East Infirmary at Princes Street, she repeated the charge but again failed to turn up at Thames Magistrates Court to prosecute.

Elizabeth appeared before the court on a number of charges of drunk and disorderly, or drunk and incapable, and on 15th July 1888, she was taken by a police constable to Poplar Workhouse from the Limehouse district and ordered to attend court the next day. On that occasion, Montague Williams, magistrate, discharged her without a fine. Her last entry in the court records shows that she failed to appear for a charge on the 3rd September.

During the evening of Saturday 29th September, Elizabeth was seen in the kitchen of 32 Flower and Dean Street by fellow lodgers Catherine Lane and Thomas Bates until she left at about 7.30 p.m.

Later that night a woman fitting her description was seen in the vicinity of Berner Street off Commercial Road, with various clients. A greengrocer Matthew Packer sold some grapes from his shop at 44 Berner Street, to a man in her company.

P.C. William Smith, 425H walked his usual beat up Berner Street at 12.30 a.m. and saw a woman he later believed to be her with a man opposite Dutfield's Yard, that adjoined the International Workingmen's Educational Club for Jewish Socialists. That night the members took part in a discussion.

Israel Schwartz, a local resident, turned into Berner Street from Commercial Road at 12.45 a.m. on his way home. When he reached the gateway at the entrance to Dutfield's Yard he witnessed an incident that he was sure involved a woman he later identified at the mortuary as Elizabeth Stride and a man. Schwartz saw the man speak to the woman then physically throw her down on the footway. When he crossed over to the other side of the street, he saw another man lighting a pipe that he believed followed him for a short distance. The first man called out Lipski a common anti-semitic insult, but it was unclear as to whether he addressed it to Schwartz or to the second man. The man who accosted Stride was described by Schwartz as 5ft 5ins tall, aged about 30, with a fair complexion, full face, brown hair, and a small brown moustache, and broad shoulders. He wore a dark jacket and trousers, and black cap with a peak.

At approximately 1.00 a.m., Louis Diemshutz, steward of the club, drove his pony and cart through the open gates into Dutfield's Yard. A hesitant reaction from the pony caused Diemshutz to discover a woman lying close to the club wall. Once entering the club he alerted members to the find, then returned outside with amongst others a man named Jacobs, and found that the woman's throat was cut. Many of the club members then ran off in different directions to attract police assistance and brought P.C. Henry Lamb, 252H to the scene of the crime. At around 1.16 a.m., Dr William Blackwell arrived and confirmed the cut to the throat was the cause of death.

The inquest took place on the 1st, 2nd, 3rd, 5th and 23rd October, with Coroner Wynne E. Baxter presiding.

Elizabeth Stride was 5ft 5ins tall, with a slender figure, blue eyes, dark brown curly hair, a straight nose, oval face, a pale complexion, and with all her teeth absent on the left lower jaw. Mr North of Poplar, said that she was nicknamed Mother Gum on account of a peculiarity of the top lip, which, when she laughed, showed the whole of the upper gum.

Her nickname used at the Spitalfields lodging houses was Long Liz, and she was a very popular good-natured and hard working lodger. She was also considered to be a good cook, and expert in the use of a sewing machine, knitting and all kinds of needlework.

Her age was 44 when she died on Sunday 30th September 1888, and she was buried in a public grave No 15509 on the 6th October at East London Cemetery in Plaistow.

Her nephew, P.C. Walter Stride, 385W briefly attended the inquest to confirm identification.

CATHERINE EDDOWES

Murdered on the same night as Elizabeth Stride by the hand of a killer that would afterwards become known as Jack the Ripper, Catherine Eddowes holds a unique place in the affections of many people who study the case. Her life story and that of her daughter Annie reads like the script of a play, it has all the elements of drama, tragedy and comedy, and Catherine holds centre stage for forty-six years from being the family favourite as a child to the family embarrassment as an adult. Yet, hundreds of people crowded the streets in 1888 to show their respect for this chirpy girl from the black country. Catherine Eddowes did not live to an age which we regard today as old age, but live she certainly did.

She was born on Thursday 14th April 1842 the daughter of George and Catherine Eddowes at Graisley Green, Wolverhampton in Staffordshire. She was the last child born to the couple in the Midlands. George was born in 1808 to Thomas and Mary Eddowes in Wolverhampton. He married Catherine Evans on the 13th August 1832 at nearby Bushbury. In Wolverhampton, Catherine became a cook at the Peacock Hotel, while husband George worked at the Old Hall Works. After the wedding they began to live at Graisley Green, and had five children before Catherine, named Alfred, Harriet, Emma, Eliza and Elizabeth.

George took his family down the country from Wolverhampton to London a year later, and the family reached the city on a barge up the River Thames. He worked as a tinplate worker and obtained employment with Perkins and Sharpus of Bell Court, Cannon Street in the City of London. He probably lost his job at a later date when the workers went on strike?

The first child in the family to be born in the south of England, was born on the 9th December 1844 and named Thomas. The family lived at 4 Baden Place, Crosby Row in Bermondsey. Another son George was born two years later, and in 1849 a boy John was born in January at their new address of 35 West Street, but died aged only 2 months on 18th March. Cause of death was certified as cyanosis, convulsions.

Little Catherine attended Dowgate Charity School in the City, and also earned herself the affectionate nickname of chick. Big sister Emma Eddowes later described the young Catherine as a lively little thing, warm-hearted and entertaining, but in 1850 she was no longer the youngest girl. Sarah Ann Eddowes was born that year, and appeared with the family on the census of 1851 at 35 West Street. The only absentees being Harriet and Emma who had left home to go into domestic service.

In 1852, another girl Mary (Ann) Eddowes was born, and the seven Eddowes girls were collectively known as the seven sisters. The last child, number twelve, was a son called William born in 1854, but he died after only 4 months of life from convulsions. In Victorian Britain, a tragic loss would quite often be followed by more tragedy, and the Eddowes family was a prime example of the way in which the cold and brutal hand of fate could turn a happy working class family into a broken and devastated family within only three years.

Wife and mother Catherine Eddowes died aged 42 on the 17th November 1855 after suffering with phthisis better known as tuberculosis of the lungs for eight months. The family was living at 7 Winters Square, and the tears were only just beginning to be wiped away when their father George passed away two years later aged 49. A death certificate cannot be found for him but it's not unlikely that he died of TB the same as his wife. Just prior to his death, George attended his daughter Elizabeth's wedding on 21st September 1857. Elizabeth married a labourer Thomas Charles Fisher at St Paul's Church in Bermondsey. George put his mark on the register. During many years following the Fisher's had at least nine children Elizabeth, Charles William, Harriet, Eliza, Joseph, Amelia, Thomas, Alfred and Robert.

On the 9th December, the younger Eddowes children George, Sarah and Mary was admitted as orphans to Bermondsey Workhouse. Their brother Thomas went in the next day. Two weeks later on the 26th December, Thomas, George and Mary, was admitted into the Industrial School (On census called the South Metropolitan District School in Sutton). Children were usually sent to Industrial Schools by a magistrate to learn a trade.

The three eldest sisters Harriet, Emma, and Eliza, all lived on the north side of the river, and after their parents died, Harriet wrote to her aunt Elizabeth Eddowes in Wolverhampton to see whether she could get sister Catherine a situation. The aunt duly obliged and the mistress at the house where Emma worked as a domestic servant at Lower Craven Place in Kentish Town, very generously paid Kate's fare back to her home town.

The eldest brother, Alfred Eddowes, was an ill man subject to fits and the elder sisters took care of him too. Faced with such dreadful circumstances to which the family was forced to cope with since the death of their parents, we can only admire the way in which Harriet and Emma took control and tried to make the best out of a bad situation for all of their siblings. In 1858, Sarah followed her brothers and sister into the Industrial School on the 8th January.

Eliza Eddowes married on the 23rd January 1859 to James Gold at St Barnabas Church, King Square in Finsbury. They lived at 5 and 20 Rahere Street in Goswell Road, and Gold worked as a butcher. Eliza later gave birth to one son and called him George. The boy George Eddowes left the Industrial School on the 7th November to go on trial to a shoemaker Mr Tebbuts of 5 Union Road, Cobourg Road in the Old Kent Road. Thomas left on 15th November to join the Band of the 45th Regiment of Infantry (The Sherwood Foresters) stationed at Preston in Lancashire. Private No. 287, Thomas Eddowes, gave his trade as shoemaker on the 19th, aged 14 years and 11 months. Emma Eddowes married James Jones a tallow chandler on the 11th November 1860 at St Barnabas Church. The Jones' had at least six children Louisa, Emma, George, James, Harriet, and Joseph.

On the 1861 census, aunt Elizabeth Eddowes lived with her husband William and their three children at 50 Bilston Street in Wolverhampton, and their niece named Cath was described as working as a scourer. According to another aunt Sarah Croot the wife of Jesse (in 1881 lived at 36 Bilston Street), Catherine worked as a tinplate stamper at the Old Hall Works in Wolverhampton where uncle William worked. Her brother George Eddowes aged 14 was an errand boy and lived with his eldest sister Harriet and her lover Robert Carter Garrett at 174 Goswell Street in Finsbury. Mary Eddowes was a scholar at the school in Sutton, and Sarah was probably there too.

Thomas Eddowes was a 16 year old private on the census based at the 45th Regiment North Camp at Aldershot in Kent. But that year he was discharged from the regiment because he was considered unfit for further military service. J. Leary the regimental surgeon wrote a medical report on the discharge certificate that stated:

This boy was enlisted a year and a half since to be trained as a musician, but from the delicacy of his chest he has been exempted from playing on a wind instrument. He has been frequently in hospital under the head of asthenia and as it is not likely he will ever make an effective soldier, he is brought forward for discharge.

At Chatham on 5th August the Principal Medical Officer observes:

Having examined Private Thomas Eddowes, I am of the opinion he is unfit for further service in consequence of tendency to pulmonary consumption.

On his discharge at Chatham on the 27th August, he was described as 16 years and 8 months, 4ft 5½ ins tall, with a fair complexion, hazel eyes, and dark brown hair. Under the heading of marks or scars the certificate said that he had been cupped on left breast. It seems very doubtful that Thomas lived for very long after his army discharge?

On 14th October 1861, Private No.350, Thomas Quinn, was discharged from the 1st Battalion of the 18th Royal Irish Regiment at Dublin. The soldier was also known as Thomas Conway but not as it seems to his regiment.

His discharge certificate records that he was born in the parish of Kilgever, Louisburgh in the county of Mayo in Ireland. He joined the regiment at the age of 20 on the 9th October 1857 at Beverley in Yorkshire. He spent two years and eighty two days serving in Bombay and Madras in India. He possessed one good conduct badge. The Musters for the 10th October to the 31st December 1860 revealed that he was staying in the Royal Hospital, Kilmainham in Dublin.

John Collins, MD, wrote in the medical report on the discharge certificate:

This man is recommended for discharge in consequence of physical debility, and constitutional infirmity, the result of former illness principally Rheumatism and Chronic Bronchitis. Had been invalided from India with disease of the heart, which he has suffered since his arrival at this station. The disease is partially if not entirely attributable to military service and climate, not to intemperance or other vice.

The Principal Medical Officer at Dublin simply added on 5th October that he was unfit for further service. When he was discharged after four years and six days service he was described as aged 24, 5ft 5ins, with a fresh complexion, grey eyes, and light brown hair. He was a labourer by trade and intended to reside in Beverley in Yorkshire. The back page appears to refer to payments made to him over the years, two of which mention Coventry. He put his mark on the certificate but it is unclear as to whether his name was really Thomas Quinn or Thomas Conway because there was a Colour Sergeant Thomas Conway in the regiment from whom he could have borrowed the name?

Catherine was unable to keep her job for long when she was found to be stealing, so she ran away in about 1862 to live with another uncle Thomas Eddowes at The Brick Hill, Bagot Street in Birmingham. He was a boot and shoemaker by trade, but was once a pugilist. Catherine obtained work as a tray polisher in Legge Street. She then returned to Wolverhampton to live with her grandfather Thomas, and then went back to Birmingham again where it was believed that she first met with Thomas Conway. By that time he was a hawker, but drew a pension from his regiment. She had his initials TC tattooed on her forearm in blue ink and always told people that they were legally married. They would spend their time as common-law husband and wife going from place to place selling chapbooks written by Conway.

Their first child together was named Catherine Ann Conway and born on the 18th April 1863 at Yarmouth Workhouse in Norfolk. Thomas worked as a general labourer, and the mother registered her child on the 13th May under the name of Catherine Conway and gave her address as the workhouse. The girl would later in life become known as Annie Conway. In 1888, Catherine's sister Emma Jones alleged that Catherine might have given birth to another daughter who died and other children who were probably not Conway's?

Catherine's grandfather, Thomas Eddowes, died on the 2nd November 1865 at Bilston Street in Wolverhampton. He was 83 and had worked as a tin ware stamper. The cause of death was an effusion on the brain and his son William of 50 Bilston Street was in attendance. Nowhere was it recorded as to whether she went to the funeral or not?

What she could not allow herself to miss though was the execution of her criminal cousin Christopher Charles Robinson aged 18, who was hanged at Stafford gaol in 1866 for the murder of his fiancée Harriet Seager in Wolverhampton. In fact, Catherine and Thomas seized the opportunity for moneymaking by selling a gallows ballad about her cousin's misfortunate as they mingled amongst the four thousand strong crowd. (Story first discovered by Kate Amy mentioned in Ripperana of 1995. Thanks to Robert McLaughlin). Robinson was born on the 15th May 1847, the son of Mary Ann late Colbourne, formerly Eddowes, and husband Christopher Robinson at North Street in Wolverhampton. The couple had one other son together, and, according to the Wolverhampton Journal on the 2nd September 1865, the father worked as a coal dealer and blacksmith and occupied a premises on Market Hall. She left £4,000 in her will, the executors being Reuben Robinson, and Josiah Fisher who lived at Sidney Street. It was at Fisher's home that the murder took place.

The Times on the 10th January 1866, gave details from the trial. On the 26th August of the previous year, Robinson cut the girl's throat with a razor and left her for dead on the floor of the scullery. She had earlier spurned his attempt to kiss her and Robinson was seen as he struck her with his open hand. After the attack on Seager, he made a vain attempt at suicide by deliberately cutting his own throat three times with the razor. He was stopped from going any further and a surgeon arrived and saved his life. Seager's Inquest took place at Graisley Brook Inn. Part of Robinson's defence at the trial was a claim that he was insane when he committed the murder, because insanity was hereditary in his family and his half-sister was in a lunatic asylum. But insanity could not be proven, and Robinson went to the gallows with the words, "Lord Jesus, receive my spirit."

Mary Eddowes aged 15 left the Industrial School on the 18th April 1867 and entered into domestic service for a Mr McDougall at 11 Brooklyn Terrace, Kings Road, in Peckham. Then back to the Industrial School on the 6th August before working from the 26th August as a servant to Mr and Mrs Bolton at 45 Russell Street in Rotherhithe. Robert Carter Garrett finally made an honest woman of Harriet Eddowes on the 6th October when they married at St Barnabas Church in Finsbury. They lived together at 17 Fann Street, Robert worked as a carman and Harriet a fancy bag maker. Meanwhile, sister Mary was back at the school again on the 16th November.

By 1868, Catherine and Thomas took clean and comfortable lodgings at Westminster in London, and a son Thomas was born there but the birth was not registered. From that time on, Emma Jones saw her sister frequently and knew about her alcoholism. Catherine always cried when she met with her and said, I wish I was like you. She occasionally left home too.

Mary Eddowes continued her domestic service tour of Southern England when on the 3rd February she worked for a watchmaker called Harthuis of 5 Park Terrace in Sutton. She was back at the school again on the 18th February, only to leave again on the 4th July for service with Mrs Jessie of 10 Gloster Terrace, Albany Road in Camberwell. Sarah Ann Eddowes returned to the Bermondsey Workhouse from the Industrial School on the 13th July, while Mary was yet again back at the school on the 14th August before going on to work for Mrs Simmonds on the 6th October at 30 Surrey Street in Camberwell. The next year, Mary was back at the school on the 5th January, but left there for what was probably the last time to work in service for Thomas Harress of 25 Cornwell Road, Brixton.

A destitute Alfred Eddowes was admitted from Newington on the 19th October 1870 to St George's Workhouse, Mint Street in St Saviour. His occupation was given as a labourer. Sarah Ann Eddowes fared even worse and was admitted on the 26th October to Caterham Asylum for Imbeciles from St Olave's Union, Bermondsey. Elizabeth Fisher of 4 Acacia Terrace in Abbey Wood was named as the informant. Two of her sons, one being Charles William of 1 Down's Place in Plumstead, also appeared on the register. Sarah's last address was with her sister Emma at 16 Bridgewater Gardens, Aldersgate in London.

Writer and researcher Chris Scott managed to track down Catherine Eddowes 1871 census entry at 1 Queen Street in Southwark. She was named Catherine Conway and worked as a laundress. Thomas Conway gave his age as 36 and worked as a pedlar. Their daughter Catherine A. Conway was aged 7, and son Thomas aged 3. The census also records Harriet Garrett and Emma Jones still living at their same addresses in Finsbury and the City, but Elizabeth Fisher had moved on to Walbridge Street in Greenwich. Mary Eddowes was a servant to the Glanville family at Portland Terrace in Rotherhithe. The less fortunate Sarah remained a patient at the Caterham Asylum.

Alfred George Conway, Catherine's last child, was born on the 15th August 1873 at St George's Workhouse, Mint Street in St Saviour. She gave her address as 119 Kent Street, and the child was christened at the workhouse before mother and son were discharged on the 26th August. She also gave the address of 20 or 120 Kent Street on registration.

Harriet Garrett was widowed when her husband Robert died aged 40 in 1874. Two years later, Alfred Eddowes was back in the workhouse in Mint Street on 13th December from 294 Kent Street, renamed Tabard Street, and was discharged on the 20th. The last time Emma Jones met with Catherine was in about 1877 at Christmas time. It was evident from her blackened eyes that she had suffered from Conway's brutality. Eleven years later, Elizabeth Fisher also accused Conway of beating their sister.

Alfred left the workhouse on the 11th March 1878, and had two more admissions from the 3rd September to the 7th October, and from the 15th October. His address 64 Tabard Street. He left the workhouse again on the 20th January 1879, but was back for two further admissions on the 27th January and the 13th September. Address Church lodging house, Tabard Street. Alfred was at the workhouse the next year on 24th February, but after that disappears from the records and was likely to have died homeless and could be registered as an unknown male?

Catherine's uncle William Eddowes in Wolverhampton, died aged 61 on 6th December 1879 in the presence of his wife Elizabeth at South Staffordshire Hospital. Cause of death was given as senile gangrene, pneumonia.

The 1881 census, revealed Catherine, Thomas and their family living at 71 Lower George Street in Chelsea. Daughter Catherine Ann was not on the census but that was probably due to a mistake by the enumerator who forgot to put her name down? Both sons attended school. Eliza Gold by then a widow, began living in the Spitalfields area and cohabited with a man from Essex named Charles Frost on the top floor of 6 Thrawl Street in Spitalfields. Frost was a Wesleyan and worked as a waterside labourer and sold farthing books in Liverpool Street. Sister Emma still lived the City area at 3 Paul's Alley, and Elizabeth had moved to 35 New Hackcliffe Street in Greenwich, her son Charles William had married a girl Eliza but remained living at his parents home.

That same year, the inevitable happened and Catherine and Thomas parted, the pensioner took his sons with him and blamed her drinking habits. Catherine followed her sister and found her way to Spitalfields and sometimes turned to prostitution, while at other times earned money working for the Jewish community in and around Brick Lane. She met and began living with a labourer-market porter John Kelly at 55 Flower and Dean Street, where she became a popular figure with other lodgers. He was described as a quiet and inoffensive man, and her friends knew her as Mrs Kelly, but she regularly used and preferred the name Kate Conway. She was charged on the 21st September 1881 at the Thames Magistrates Court with being drunk and disorderly and using obscene language, but was discharged without a fine by Magistrate Thomas William Saunders.

An unmarried Catherine Ann Conway aged 19 gave birth to a boy Louis in about 1882, likely to have been the first son of Louis Phillips from Waterloo. A second followed on the 22nd September 1884, called Catherine Phillips whilst the parents lived at 317 Weston Street in Southwark. The mother registered the child as Catherine Phillips.

Catherine Eddowes younger brother George died of a cerebral haemorrhage aged 39 on the 5th March 1885 at the Hemel Hempstead Workhouse in Hertfordshire. His occupation was given as a labourer but the record also pointed towards the possibility of him being a tramp. His death was witnessed by the Master J. Burnett, and he was buried on the 7th March at St Mary's Churchyard in Hemel Hempstead (Thanks to Nick Connell).

Louis Phillips finally realised it was time to marry the mother of his two children, and marry they did on the 3rd August 1885 at St Mary Magdalene Church in Southwark. Annie Conway as she called herself lived with Louis and the kids at 14 Townsend Street on the Old Kent Road. Louis worked as lampblack packer. Annie visited her mother around this time at the lodging house in Flower and Dean Street, and Grandmother Kate attended her daughter's confinement a year later when Annie lived at 22 King Street in Bermondsey. It was later alleged by Annie at her mother's inquest, that they last met when her son William Phillips born on the 10th August 1886, was only 1 week old. Annie said in 1888 that she chose to have nothing further to do with her mother because of her persistence in applying to her for money, and Thomas Conway kept the whereabouts of the two boys from her for the same reason. However, Annie registered her son on the 26th October, again calling herself Catherine Phillips whilst still living at the same address, so obviously she did not feel the need to escape her mother's constant demands until a good two months after the boy's birth.

In 1887, Conway and one of his sons stayed with Annie for a time when she lived at 15 Anchor Street in Southwark Park Road. Conway left on bad terms with his daughter before Annie and her family moved on to nearby 12 Dilston Grove. She was employed as a domestic servant at Kensington.

At 5.15 p.m., on Tuesday 14th June, Catherine as Kate Conway was admitted to the Whitechapel Workhouse Infirmary with a burn on her foot and sent to Ward E2. She gave her religion as Roman Catholic due to her associations with Irishmen Thomas Conway and John Kelly, and was discharged from the Infirmary six days later on the 20th June. From then on, she continued to spend her life in the common lodging houses of Spitalfields and casual wards of East London, only leaving the area during the hop-picking season.

During the summer of 1888, Catherine and John Kelly chose to go hop-picking to Hunton near Coxheath in Kent. In Maidstone, she purchased a pair of boots from Arthur Pash of the High Street, and a jacket from Mr Edmetts' pawnbroker shop. They returned to London on the 28th September, and in the Houndsditch the next day the couple parted for the last time at 2.00 p.m. having spent all their money on food and drink. At 8.30 p.m., Catherine was found drunk on the pavement outside 29 Aldgate High Street by City Police Constable Louis Robinson, 931 and a crowd began to gather. Robinson attempted to stand her up against the shutters, but being unsuccessful in the attempt he was assisted by City P.C. George Simmons who helped take her to Bishopsgate Police Station where City Sergeant Byfield put her in a cell to sober up.

City P.C. George Hutt, 968 released her at 1.00 a.m. after she gave a false name and address of Mary Ann Kelly, 6 Fashion Street, and left the police station with the words, Good night, old cock. Just after 1.30 a.m., three men left the Imperial Club at Duke's Place in the City of London. Joseph Lawende, Joseph Hyam Levy and Harry Harris saw a man and a woman standing talking by the entrance of Church Passage that led into Mitre Square. Lawende later identified the woman as Catherine Eddowes by the clothes she was wearing. He described the man as 5ft 7-8 ins tall, aged about 30, with a fair complexion and moustache, and of medium build. He had the appearance of a sailor and wore a pepper-and-salt coloured loose jacket, grey cloth cap with a peak, and a reddish neckerchief.

City P.C. James Harvey, 964 entered Church Passage on his beat at about 1.40 a.m. and saw no one. Only five minutes later City P.C. Edward Watkins walked into Mitre Square on his regular beat from

Mitre Street and discovered the mutilated body of a woman lying in the virtual darkness of the southwest corner. Watkins ran to a nearby warehouse where he found the night watchman George James Morris who after taking a look at the body went off to search for further police assistance. The first doctor on the scene Dr George Sequeira confirmed that life was extinct.

At 2.55 a.m., a portion of bloodstained apron taken from the victim was found at 108-119 Goulsten Street Buildings by Police Constable Alfred Long, 254A. Above on the wall was the words written in chalk, The Juwes are the men that will not be blamed for nothing. Whether the writing was the work of the murderer we will never know because Metropolitan Police Commissioner Charles Warren had the words removed for fear of a riot against the local Jewish population. Dr Frederick Gordon Brown performed a post-mortem later that day at Golden Lane Mortuary. The throat had been deeply cut, face disfigured, body dreadfully mutilated, and the left kidney and womb removed.

John Kelly identified her body, she was aged 46 when she died, the second murder victim in the early hours of the 30th September. Eliza Gold still lived at 6 Thrawl Street and her son George, a woodchopper, lived there too and also a little girl aged 10 named Emily Downing. She was probably the child of Charles Frost and Elizabeth Downing the former deputy of 53 Flower and Dean Street? Eliza rose from her sick bed and accompanied a detective and her son and a young woman named Lizzie Griffiths to identify her sister's body at the mortuary. Eliza was described as a middle-sized woman with a face that retained a pleasant and agreeable appearance.

After a time, Annie Phillips came forward, and with John Kelly and Eliza Gold, gave evidence at her mother's inquest. Coroner Samuel F. Langham conducted the inquest on the 4th and the 11th October at the Coroners Court in Golden Lane. Eliza Gold pointed out Annie to her sisters especially Elizabeth Fisher who had never once met with her niece. She was five months pregnant but it did not seem to show, because this fact was not mentioned in any of the press reports. A book called The News from Whitechapel by DiGrazia, Chisholm and Yost mentions that at the end of the inquest the jury presented their fees to Annie Phillips. The funeral took place on the 8th October and was attended by members of the family and John Kelly. Her body in a elm coffin, was placed in an open glass hearse which was pulled by two black horses each wearing a large black plume on its forehead. She was buried in a public grave at the City of London Cemetery in Ilford.

Catherine Eddowes was 5ft tall, with hazel eyes, a dark complexion and a very thick upper lip, and auburn hair. She was hard working and generous to her friends, very jolly-often singing. When she died she was wearing amongst other things, a black straw bonnet, black cloth jacket trimmed around the collar and cuffs with imitation fur, a brown linsey bodice, a dark green chintz skirt patterned with michaelmas daisies and golden lilies. A pair of men's lace up boots, and one piece of red gauze silk worn as a neckerchief.

Thomas Conway eventually crept out of hiding after the inquest with his two sons to remove any suspicion against him, and met with his daughter for the first time in fifteen to eighteen months. He lived at 43 York Street in Westminster, and had seen Catherine in the streets once or twice since their separation but avoided her as best he could, and was aware that she lived with John Kelly.

Emma Jones was interviewed by The Standard on the 4th October and gave her address as 20 Bridgewater Place. Her retired uncle Thomas Eddowes aged 77 who lived at 112 Moland Street in Birmingham, was reported in the Midland Evening News on the 5th October. He had not seen Kate for at least twenty years, when he was informed of her murder in London. He was greatly affected by the news and died soon afterwards in the presence of his wife Charlotte on 18th October. Cause of death was senility, dropsy (cardiac). John Kelly became ill with a kidney ailment and a bad cough, and was admitted on the 29th November to Whitechapel Workhouse Infirmary with laryngitis.

Annie Phillips gave birth to her fourth child Ellen on the 20th February 1889 at 21 The Grange in Bermondsey. She registered the child on the 25th March and that time called herself Annie. A fifth and final child followed a year later on 19th May and was called Thomas, the family lived at 1 Paulin Street in Bermondsey but by the 1891 census the family had moved again. Living in two rooms at 13 Dix's Place in Bermondsey, Louis brother George was also staying there.

Thomas Conway lived at 9 Parker Street in St Margaret's Westminster in one room with his son (Alfred) George aged 17 and an employed general labourer. His other son Thomas aged 24 was employed as a night watchman at the lodging house run by Thomas Groves at 12-14 Lombard Street in Southwark.

Harriet Garrett was admitted to the Holborn Infirmary at Archway Road in Islington and was one of the sick patients on the census, before being admitted later on the 15th September from St Luke's to the Holborn Workhouse at Mitcham. Her occupation was given at the infirmary as a paper bag maker but her calling at the workhouse was washing. Harriet was discharged from the workhouse on the 22nd August 1892, but returned on the 25th. Emma Jones was recorded as a relative, she lived at 6a Shaftesbury Place in 1891 at St Botolph Aldersgate, and her three sons had work but still lived at home. Elizabeth Fisher and family had moved house again to 33 Commerell Street in Greenwich, but her sister Eliza Frost, formerly Gold, continued to suffer from her illness while living with Charles Frost at 58 Flower and Dean Street.

On the 10th January 1893, Eliza was admitted at 5.00 p.m. to the Whitechapel Infirmary and sent to Ward A3. The cause of the admission was probably a chest infection but she died the next day aged 55 or 56. Coroner Wynne E. Baxter conducted the inquest on the 16th January, and he certified various reasons after post mortem for the cause of death as sudden, heart disease and bronchitis accelerated by alcoholism, and want of food, natural.

Harriet probably unaware of her sister's death left the Holborn Workhouse on the 31st October 1893 and was re-admitted on the 1st November. Harriet died of apoplexy on 17th November 1898 at the workhouse aged about 64 or 65 and Grace Norman, the Matron of the workhouse registered the death.

The next census in 1901, Annie Phillips and her family had moved on again to 6 Haddon House, Russell Place in Southwark, but eldest son Louis was not with them. Thomas Conway had also moved down the street to 19 Parker Street. He was a hawker of curtains and his son Thomas lived with him and was employed as a parish sweeper, vestry? Emma Jones lived at 33 Bastwick Street in St Luke's and her aged husband still worked as a glass packer. Elizabeth had been widowed the year prior to the census, so lived with her daughter Amelia and her soldier husband John Thorpe and their three children at 1 Down's Place in Plumstead.

Sadly, Thomas the eldest son of Catherine Eddowes, died aged 36 on the 31st October 1903 at St George's Infirmary, Fulham Road. in Chelsea. He had worked as a labourer and was still living with his father at Parker Street when he died. J.E. Coulson M.R.C.S. certified the death as pulmonary tuberculosis, and H.W. Webster the Medical Superintendent of the infirmary was the informant.

Every cloud has a silver lining, and on the 8th June 1908 Catherine Phillips probably became the first grandchild of Catherine Eddowes to be married? The groom was Thomas Hall a labourer and the ceremony took place at St Mary Magdalene Church, Massinger Street in Southwark. They both lived at 16 Madron Street, and siblings Ellen and Thomas Phillips was the witnesses. A month later on the 31st July, grandfather Thomas Conway alias Quinn died aged about 80 at St Olave's Workhouse, Parish Street in Bermondsey. Death was recorded as senility and demented, occupation and address as army pensioner of the 18th Royal Irish, Identity No.350 of Lynton Mews.

Catherine Hall gave birth the next year to an auburn haired daughter and called her Catherine Sarah on the 15th April at Camberwell, and in the years following she had three sons Thomas, William and Joseph Lewis. In 1911, Louis Phillips first appeared on the electoral register at a dwelling house 40 Westcott Street, Tabard Street in Southwark.

Thomas Phillips married on Christmas Day at St Paul's Church in Bermondsey. His bride was Emily Jackson and they both lived at 18 Staple Street. He was a lampblack packer. Four children followed, Thomas Lewis in 1912, William Henry and a twin (both died in 1914), and Emily Annie born a year later when Thomas and his wife lived in his parents house at 40 Westcott Street. His sister Ellen Phillips married a labourer Joseph William Wells on the 4th August 1912 at the same church as her sister Catherine. The couple also lived at the same address in Madron Street. A year later, a girl named Ellen Mary Ann Wells was born, and then followed another girl, Violet, in 1914 at Bermondsey, then a boy Joseph Lewis born at Bagshot Street in Southwark, but he died. Then came Catherine Annie Wells, and a boy Thomas Lewis who current family believe committed suicide at 18 during World War Two? Then lastly, a girl Rose Lillian who died at 1 year old.

When the call to arms came in World War One, Thomas Phillips enlisted on 26th June 1916 into the 2nd/24th (County of London Regiment) Battalion TF (The Queens) at Kennington. His service took him to Egypt where he died prematurely of an abscess on the liver on the 19th August 1918. He was buried at the Cairo War Memorial Cemetery as Private No. 721750 part of the European Expeditionary

Force, and was posthumously awarded both the British War Medal and Victory Medal. He was listed as an absent voter for 40 Westcott Street. Likewise, Joseph William Wells was listed for Southwark as warrant number 104505 Stoker on H.M.S. Saripta.

Family stories suggest that brothers Louis and William Phillips also died in World War One? If the stories were true then Annie Phillips surely could not have believed that her grief would continue when war was finally over, but it was just the beginning of her woe. On 4th November 1919, Catherine Hall died aged 35 at 7 Crown Street in Camberwell. Cause of death was certified by D.A. Birrell LRCH as tuberculosis of the lungs for three months, and debility, heart failure.

Her husband Thomas was left with the children but would eventually re-marry. A year later, Annie lost her husband, Louis died of a cerebral haemorrhage aged 57 on the 23rd August at Dulwich Hospital. More than likely, Annie had not met with her aunt Elizabeth Fisher since her mother's inquest so was probably unaware that she died on the 18th December of senile decay, address given as 72 Earl Street in Plumstead. A widowed Annie Phillips was not left alone at the house, a woman named Emily Wright started living with her in 1923, and was no doubt a source of great comfort for her during her troubles that were not yet over .

On the 21st December 1924, Ellen Wells died of cancer of the cervix aged 35 at Dulwich Hospital, her mother Annie was now left with the task of helping to bring up both of her deceased daughters children. In the course of 61 years of life she had lost a mother to Jack the Ripper, a father and brother to poverty, and then within ten years lost a husband, probably all three sons to war, and two daughters to premature deaths. If she was a believer in a God, she must have felt it was time for him to show some much needed mercy. Her brother-in-law George Phillips returned to live in her house again and like Emily Wright offered the emotional support required.

The forgotten member of the family, Sarah Ann Eddowes, Catherine Eddowes younger sister died on 26th February 1928 at the Caterham Asylum for Imbeciles after spending almost fifty-eight years of her life incarcerated there. Cause of death given by the Superintendent J. Leslie Gordon was senile decay.

Annie was last named on the electoral register at 40 Westcott Street in Southwark in 1933. During the most recent years, three more people had stayed in the house with her Susan and Rose Phillips, and Thomas Ramsey. She died aged 80 of senile myocardial degeneration on the 15th July at Lambeth Hospital. Her last occupation was given as a paper sorter (retired), and she had lived at 107 Chaucer House, Tabard Street in Southwark.

Annie outlived all of her family and she coped admirably with terrible tragedy to live to a grand old age. In the end, she died when her home address was in the same street, namely Tabard Street, where her mother and Jack the Ripper victim Catherine Eddowes had lived seventy years before!

MARY JANE KELLY

Mary Jane Kelly has remained a mystery for the last one hundred and twenty years in the same way as the murderer known throughout the world as Jack the Ripper. The killer's face is likely to stay hidden behind the veil of anonymity, but with Kelly we can hope that the young girl whose body was destroyed in a dingy little room in Spitalfields will someday be found in the records. The scant details that a biographer has to rely upon are her own somewhat dubious accounts told to her lover Joseph Barnett and friends in the East End.

She alleged that she was the daughter of John Kelly born about 1863-1864 in Limerick in Ireland. There was six brothers and one sister. Her parents was said to be fairly well-off and when she was a child they travelled across the Irish Sea to live in Carmarthenshire in Wales, where her father found employment as a gaffer at an ironworks. Her sister, who was very fond of her, lived with an aunt and would travel with materials from one market to another. A brother named Henry Kelly (aka John or Johnto) served in the 2nd Battalion Scots Guards.

When Mary was sixteen, she married a collier named Davis or Davies who was killed in a explosion between one to three years after the marriage. The widow Davis then went to Cardiff to stay with a cousin who was believed to be the cause of her resorting to prostitution. For eight to nine months she was an inmate of the Cardiff Infirmary for an unspecified reason.

Kelly first arrived in London about 1884 and went to a madam of a brothel in the West End where a gentleman asked her to go to France with him. She was in France barely a fortnight and decided she did not like the place and returned to London.

She first entered the East End to live with a Mrs Buki or Baki in St George's Street in St George's-in-the-East. One of her friends was Lizzie Williams possibly a Welsh woman and maybe the origin of Kelly's Welsh life history?

Research carried out by various authors and researchers has failed to prove any of the stories she told about living in Carmathenshire, the marriage to Davis when she was aged 16, or that her brother Henry served in the 2nd Battalion Scots Guards. In my own research, I made a list of all the men named Kelly in the Muster Books for the 2nd Battalion Scots Guards from 1885 to mid-1888 at the Public Records Office in London. There was four James Kelly's, two Patrick's, two Michael's, one William, one Robert, one Thomas, and a P. and M. Kelly, none of which enthused me enough to believe that I had found Mary's brother. Other name options were O'Kelly, Keily or Kiely, Keilly, and Killey, again none was called Henry or John. Could it be that the man who was supposed to be Mary Jane Kelly's brother was in fact a former lover, but if so, in 1888 it was a good cover story that Barnett fell for hook, line, and sinker?

Both her landlord at Dorset Street in 1888 and a City of London missionary, told newspaper reporters that Kelly was receiving letters from her mother living in Ireland right up until the time she died. Her family could have returned to Ireland from Wales, or maybe they never left Ireland in the first place?

From Mrs Buki's house she more than likely took lodgings at 1 Breezer's Hill, Pennington Street in St George's-in-the-East. The woman there was called Mrs Carthy in newspaper reports but her real name was probably Mary McCarthy with no apparent connection to John McCarthy of Dorset Street. However, identification of Mrs Carthy or McCarthy's life history is disputed. On one occasion, Kelly's father came looking for his daughter, but she heard from her companions that he was looking for her and kept out of his way. At another time, she was closely associated with a man named Morganstone who lived near Stepney Gasworks. Authors Stewart Evans and Nick Connell made a probable identification of the family of Morganstern's in their book, The Man Who Hunted Jack the Ripper. Dutch brothers Adrienus and Maran were gas workers, and the former lived in the East End using the name Thomas Morganstern. Subsequently, Kelly had a relationship with Joseph Fleming, a mason-plasterer of Bethnal Green.

She then moved into Spitalfields and took lodgings in Thrawl Street, and in 1887 met with Joseph Barnett a porter at Billingsgate Market. It was Barnett who affectionately gave her a Frechified version of her name, Marie Jeanette. They lived together at George Street , and Paternoster Row in Dorset Street, then Brick Lane, and finally a small room 13 Miller's Court in Dorset Street.

Prior to the evening of Thursday 8th November 1888, Kelly allowed some of her female friends to stay at the room, and this was the reason for an argument that caused Barnett to leave her just over a week previous. Nonetheless, he continued to visit and give her money.

Barnett called on Kelly between 7.30-8.00 p.m., while her friend Lizzie Albrook was visiting. Kelly spent the rest of the evening drinking at a local public house, she was then seen with a client at 11.45 p.m. by a fellow Miller's Court lodger Mary Ann Cox and was heard singing in her room.

At about 2.00 a.m., a man who claimed to know her well named George Hutchinson, met Kelly in Commercial Street and she asked him for 6d. Hutchinson was unable to give her any money but in a short time he watched as another man approached, after they shared some light-hearted words together they headed back towards him. He stood at the Queen's Head public house as they passed, and he followed them back to Dorset Street where after a few minutes they entered the archway into Miller's Court and to Kelly's room. Hutchinson remained in Dorset Street for three quarters of an hour to see if they would come out again, but they did not, so he left. Hutchinson described the man as aged 34-35, 5ft 6ins tall, pale complexion, dark hair, moustache curled at each end, long dark coat, collar cuffs of astrakhan, dark jacket underneath, light waistcoat, thick gold chain with a red stone seal, dark trousers and button boots, gaiters, white buttons, white shirt, black tie fastened with a horseshoe pin, dark hat, turned down in middle, red kerchief. Jewish and respectable in appearance. One wonders whether Hutchinson and Kelly attended the same school for fantasists?

Meanwhile, Sarah Lewis went to stay with a Mrs Keyler on the first floor of 2 Miller's Court at a time that she later told police was around 2.30 a.m., and appeared to confirm some of the detail of events given by Hutchinson. Lewis also claimed that she heard a cry of Murder emanate from nearby just prior to 4.00 a.m. A lodger at the room above Kelly's named Elizabeth Prater might have heard the same cry after her kitten awakened her from her sleep.

At 10.45 a.m., landlord John McCarthy of 27 Dorset Street sent Thomas Bowyer to collect the rent from Mary Jane Kelly. When she failed to open the door, Bowyer looked through the broken windowpane of Kelly's room then rushed back to McCarthy and told him what he had seen. McCarthy hurried out to look himself and saw a mutilated body lying on the bed. He sent Bowyer for police assistance, but then followed on behind. Inspector Walter Beck and other officers arrived to take charge of the crime scene. When the room was entered that afternoon, clothing was found burned in the grate where a fire had also melted the solder of the spout and handle of a kettle.

Dr Thomas Bond, police surgeon, was brought to Miller's Court at 2.00 p.m. to make an examination of the body. The scene that greeted every observer would stay with them throughout their lives. In common with previous victims the throat was deeply cut, but on this occasion the killer had the ample time he needed to carry out the most horrendous butchery. He had rendered the victim's body virtually unrecognizable to those that knew her well. In the course of the savagery the killer had removed her heart and taken it away with him.

Coroner Roderick Macdonald quickly dispatched the inquest on 12th November, and the funeral of took place on the 19th. The same as with the other victims, the East End men, women, and children, came out of their homes and lined the streets in order to pay their last respects. The coffin was buried in an unmarked grave at St Patrick's Catholic Cemetery, Leytonstone.

Mary Jane Kelly was described as 5ft 7ins tall, good looking, with blue eyes, a fresh complexion, and a very good head of hair that reached to her waist. She was stout, and allegedly had two protruding false teeth in the upper jaw? A woman of smart appearance, she wore a distinctive maroon shawl and she would sell flowers to help earn a living. Her friends said she was educated and a popular character who offered sound advice to her younger friends. Out of kindness, she often invited them to stay at her room on a cold night if they was in need of shelter.

The People Newspaper of the 11th November 1888, reported that Kelly had been a friend of the previous victim Annie Chapman? According to the Evening News of the 12th November, Kelly attended meetings at a City Mission.

The Echo of the 14th November, claimed that on the day before Kelly was murdered she spoke with her landlady Mrs Elizabeth McCarthy about Jack the Ripper and said, That dreadful man! Ain't he a caution! I wonder who he'll have next?

So who was the woman murdered at Miller's Court?

When research continuously fails to provide us with the answers in the national archives, then in my view we are left with only two options:

The first is that her name really was Mary Jane Kelly, but her life history is humbug. Maybe stolen from a friend or just fictionalized Stride fashion. Her mother was probably in Ireland in 1888? Where is the record of the family in Wales? Where is the marriage to Davis or Davies at 16? Where is Henry or John/to Kelly in the 2nd Battalion Scots Guards?

The other option is that her history is true but her name is false. Mary Jane-something?

That option retains the possibility of a marriage at 16 as Mary Jane-something, and likewise her brother being a Scots Guardsman but that his real name was Henry or John/to-something?

The only problem with the second option of course is that her name might not have been Mary Jane or Kelly, nightmare scenario!

Who knows that by finding the real Mary Jane Kelly, we might just find the real Jack the Ripper?

THE MEETINGS

The first point I always have to make to anyone that asks about the victims is that none of the descendants know about the history of their murdered ancestor!

No family legends, just silence.

So many people would ask the question why contact them at all then? Well, I have always had the same answer, which is that if one of the Jack the Ripper victims had been my ancestor I would want to know. But to actually trace and contact a descendant of one of the victims was something I found difficult to talk myself into carry out. The only problem being was that I knew that someone would at some point in time, so it probably better be me.

However, it took me about eight years to go ahead with it. After all, how do you approach a descendant of a Jack the Ripper victim and tell them about their ancestor Annie Chapman and not only have to reveal that she was a prostitute, but was murdered in the most horrific way. So when in August 2001 I finally contacted a lady who I knew to be the great granddaughter of Annie, I had no idea as the first person ever to contact her as to what I could expect from the meeting?

I was able to meet the lady on the 3rd September at a South London library, she told me via email the day before that she had a picture of her grandmother Annie Georgina Chapman when she was a child and a similar one of her sister Emily Ruth. I had not told her of the family connection to Jack the Ripper because I feared I would never hear from her again, rather I decided to take it step by step.

In the library we found a place to sit, and I started off our conversation by saying to her that she could walk away anytime if she felt she didn't want to know anymore because the details would be unpleasant, thankfully she never chose to take that option. I spent the first thirty minutes explaining to her about Annie Chapman's life, and produced certificates, census material and pictures of significant places.

When I had finished, the lady brought out copies of photographs of the children she had already told me about, but while I looked at the photographs I noticed out of the corner of my eye a photograph she held in her other hand of a couple dressed in clothes from the 1860's. The lady explained that these were the parents of Annie Georgina. At first, I just sat there looking at the picture knowing that this was Annie Chapman, a Jack the Ripper victim alive and well! It would have been taken around the time of her marriage to John Chapman in 1869.

At that point, I had to conceal my excitement because I still had to inform the lady of the truth of what happened to Annie Chapman. Firstly, I told her that Annie had gone from Windsor to live in the East End of London in the 1880's. I then told her that Annie was not a murderer, but a victim of a murder, one of at least five. I then asked her if she could think of any famous murderers in the East End in the late Victorian period? Still no response, until I said, Who is the most famous murderer you can think of? Her response finally came, Jack the Ripper!

I nodded my head, and her reaction was one of only mild surprise. She said she had not known the woman, so was not bothered about being the great granddaughter of a Jack the Ripper victim and was pleased to know the truth. When I showed her a picture of Annie from the Illustrated Police News of 1888, she said it looked like her mother when she was younger. We parted after a couple of hours and the lady still communicates with me despite wishing to keep her anonymity, which I am happy to comply with fully. I recently received a description from her of Annie Georgina Chapman because for some reason I never got round to asking. She told me that Annie Georgina had blue eyes, black hair when young and was about 5 ft 3-4 ins tall, and well built. She was well spoken and spoke softly. She did not have an accent other than one coming from South London. Like her mother Annie Chapman, she was good with her hands, especially knitting.

The descendants of Mary Ann Nichols do not have a photograph of her passed down to them, but at least we can now see the faces of Mary's children Edward John and Alice Esther as adults on photographs left behind with the family. Maybe the face of Mary can be seen in them?

In April 2006, Maureen Adamson, great, great granddaughter of Mary Ann Nichols travelled the long distance to London from her home in Canada to experience the places where her ancestor had walked over a century ago. Maureen had originally found out about my work via the incomparable online database of Jack the Ripper history called Casebook, and found out about her connection to a Ripper victim via the internet.

We met at St Bride's Church in Fleet Street where Mary married William Nichols in 1864, before we were joined by Ripperologist Andy Aliffe, who went with us across London to the site formerly known as Buck's Row in Whitechapel. There Andy showed Maureen the site on which Mary's body had been found on the night she died. Maureen later said to me that she felt very uneasy in that place. After Andy departed, we made our way back to central London and walked around the now much altered streets of Shoe Lane and Fetter Lane where Mary spent her childhood. Then across Blackfriars Bridge to the Lambeth Peabody Buildings the home of the Nichols family and where two children was born and a marriage finally came to an end.

On the second day, we visited the City of London Cemetery in Ilford and laid flowers on Mary's grave, Maureen felt quite emotional standing by the last resting place of her ancestor, and was very pleased to see so many flowers left by visitors who felt equally a great sympathy for Mary. We then walked over to Catherine Eddowes grave and laid some flowers there to commemorate her 160th birthday. Back in the East End later in the day, we took a walk to the Frying Pan public house in Brick lane which Mary frequented, and look down what remains of Thrawl Street where Mary once lived. We then walked a short distance to the sign at Osborn Street and pondered for a while, here was where Mary was last seen alive before walking off to meet Jack the Ripper probably somewhere along the Whitechapel Road?

We met at Westminster Station on the third day and walked across the bridge to St Mary's Lambeth where Mary's parents married in 1840, and on a walk back to Trafalgar Square we remembered that Mary allegedly spent time there at the end of 1887 as one of the homeless. In the evening, we blended in with the crowds to hear Donald Rumbelow and his famous Ripper walk.

On Maureen's last day, I took her to the various record repositories in London in order for her to get copies from marriage registers and workhouse registers with connections to Mary's life. The visit was then over. Maureen now takes an active interest in the subject and will no doubt be back one day to retread the steps her ancestor once made.

In 2002, I started my search for the family of Catherine Eddowes,

I knew that by my own research that Catherine's daughter Annie Phillips was my only real chance of finding any information or even photographs. My research took me first down the descendants line of Catherine Phillips, Annie's eldest daughter.

Catherine Phillips had a daughter and three sons, but the daughter Catherine Sarah Hall was one of the family lines that I knew was essential to contact. By a long route, I found the address of Catherine Sarah's daughter named Josephine and sent her an introductory letter without revealing her relation to her victim ancestor. Unfortunately, the internet can unmask all, and Josephine's daughter Jan found my name on Casebook so the connection to Catherine Eddowes was made clear to them before I could reveal the truth myself. At first the lady was very upset to learn that her great, great grandmother was a Jack the Ripper victim. Only a few days before my letter arrived she had said to her husband that she could not understand why she knew nothing about her mother's ancestors. Her mother Catherine Sarah who died in the 1980's had an interest in crime history and would talk regularly with her son-in-law about crime subjects. Josephine's husband had been a police officer and attended 10 Rillington Place at the time of the arrest of serial killer John Christie. Never during the course of the conversations was there any reference made to a connection to one of Jack the Ripper's victims, because Catherine Sarah like all other Eddowes descendants was not aware of it. All she passed down to her daughter from Annie Phillips was a pair of earrings.

I spent a very pleasant afternoon at Josephine's house soon after my first contact. She told me that her uncle, now deceased, had worked at Somerset House many years ago but was unable to come up with any information about the family. There was a history in the family on her mother's side of kidney trouble, which is of interest for anyone who believes that Catherine Eddowes had Bright's disease when she died.

Looking back, she remembered being taken by her mother to Annie Phillips' house soon after she died in 1943 where her mother spoke privately out of earshot to Catherine Wells, also known as Kitty. Josephine believed that most of the property was sold off because they were all quite poor, and with it probably went the family photographs.

An interesting fact that I pointed out to her was that on the back of her mother's picture from the 1920's was the address of the photographic studio for 39 Duke Street, London EC3. The street was a short walk from Mitre Square where Catherine Eddowes was murdered. The lady herself used to get out at Aldgate Station when she worked many years ago, a coincidence that she shares with numerous relations of Eddowes who have workplaces near to Mitre Square.

Josephine has kept in regular contact with me and has generously given her time to be interviewed for a French television programme about Jack the Ripper in 2003, provided DNA for both a top Australian molecular scientist in 2005 and a British television programme about Jack the Ripper in 2006. She also telephoned the Jeremy Beadle show on LBC in 2003 to talk about her connection to Catherine Eddowes, and her daughter also gave her time to visit a well-known television medium.

The second line of research to try was that of Ellen Phillips, Annie Phillips' younger daughter. Correspondence in 2003 with Jean a daughter of Ellen's eldest child Ellen Mary Ann Wells, provided me with the photograph of Ellen Phillips and her family that is the earliest one discovered of any member of the Eddowes descendants. Jean has helped me with a good deal of information too and also with the DNA tests in 2005 and 2006. Surprisingly, initial contact with Susan the daughter of Catherine Wells in 2003 brought little result. Catherine, who has sadly died since, was the informant on Annie Phillips' death certificate, but did not have any photographs of Annie Phillips or her family. She had certainly not been aware of the relation to Catherine Eddowes, so I came to the conclusion that Annie herself destroyed any evidence of her past.

Just before Christmas of 2006, I received a very interesting email from a lady called Tracey who had contacted Susan and was told about my research. Tracey is a great granddaughter of Thomas Phillips, the youngest son of Annie Phillips, who died in World War One. It was totally unexpected because I was not aware that Thomas had married, let alone had children. His son Thomas Lewis Phillips married Cissy who gave birth to one son who died, and three daughters. Thomas Phillips' daughter Emily Annie Phillips married Albert and had four children, one named Jean married George Smith who are the parents of Tracey and her sister Penny, who are both now parents themselves.

Tracey informed me that her grandmother Emily had auburn hair the same as Catherine Eddowes, whereas Tracey herself is similar in height at only 4ft 11ins tall. Her mother Jean Smith can only remember her great grandmother Annie Phillips from her childhood as a small woman, but nothing more. Tracey works in Whitechapel near the Ripper sites and has a work colleague whose interest in the murders stretches back many years.

On the 14th July 2007, I had the great pleasure of presenting my own version of a Ripper walk for numerous descendants of Catherine Eddowes. I arranged with Tracey that we would meet at 12.00 noon, and everyone arrived on time from the older family members such as Jean Smith and her cousin Jean the daughter of Thomas Lewis Phillips. To Susan the daughter of Catherine Wells and Philip another line of Thomas Lewis Phillips, to the generation of tomorrow including Tracey's son, a little girl with ginger hair, and babies in pushchairs.

I started my walk with a very quick look at what used to be the Working Lads' Institute and the shop where the Elephant Man was put on show in Whitechapel Road. I then led them all round to what used to be Buck's Row for the Nichols murder, then talking as we go on to Berner Street and back to Whitechapel Road. At Aldgate East Station, we joked about how Catherine Eddowes was found by police on her last night lying drunk on the floor and impersonating a fire engine. We then strode on directly to Mitre Square.

We stopped at Church Passage for a photo opportunity where the family stood either side of a bit of modern graffiti which read Catherine Eddowes Square 1842-1888. When we walked over to what is known as Ripper's corner for a much needed rest on the benches by the flowerbed, I pulled out a family tree and pictures of Mitre Square and Church Passage as they used to look. Discussion then followed about the family tree and the precise position of where Catherine's body was found. Then more photographs. Tracey thought of one photo with only the female members of the group standing on Catherine's spot, which was a great idea.

The hot sun kept burning down on us, so we made for Liverpool Street Station for refreshments. An hour later, Jean Smith and Susan stayed back at the station with some of the younger members of the group, while the rest of us completed the walk at Dorset Street and Hanbury Street. A great day was had by all, and the guide was equally pleased to have remembered so much that he once thought he had forgotten long ago.

So after twenty one years of research into the lives of the Jack the

Ripper victims, is there anyone left to look for and research avenues to take in future?

Only Eliza Sarah is still to find in Mary Ann Nichols family. No-one knows what happened to her after 1901, neither a marriage or death certificate can be found to date. Maureen Adamson is interested in the family of Mary's brother Edward Walker which could yield some new finds. Maybe William Nichols' children by Rosetta Walls will have some photographs or family stories?

I would like to know what happened to Annie Chapman's son the paralysed John Alfred. Fountain Smith must have descendants around today, so at least a picture of Fountain is likely to surface in the future. Emily Latitia had no children of her own, but her step-children might have kept a picture of her and passed it down to descendants.

Although I believe that the research on Elizabeth Stride to be as complete as it's ever going to be, just maybe her brother Svante will be found in the records of another country after a life at sea.

On Catherine Eddowes, there are still some important names to track down. Her son Alfred George Conway disappeared after 1891, but hopefully will appear again on the 1911 census along with his sister's sons Louis and William Phillips, whom like Alfred George, must be traced to complete the search for the elusive family photographs. I have been in contact for some years with a lady called Mrs Stevenson who is one of Elizabeth Fisher's descendants, and she has provided me with a picture of Elizabeth's son Charles William Fisher. I hope that in time the descendants of Emma Jones and Eliza Gold could be contacted too, and perhaps we will find out what happened to their youngest sister Mary Eddowes.

And Mary Jane Kelly! Who knows?

Whatever the research finds will bring in the future, the descendants will tell us new stories, new remembrances, and hopefully reveal new photographs to add to the colourful picture that we now have of four out of the five Ripper victims. We now know that despite the fact that Nichols, Chapman and Eddowes' turbulent lives came to end in 1888, their families' lives went on. Some of the descendants married and had children, some served in World Wars and some did not come back, some lived through the swinging sixties and some saw a man walk on the moon for the first time.

Back in 1888, Mary, Annie, and Kate, walked the dimly lit streets at a time that we now commonly call Jack the Ripper's London. It resides more in fiction than in reality, but helps to feed the imagination that the film world first created.

Today, there are probably well over one hundred living direct descendants of the Jack the Ripper victims, and we might be living in the same streets as them, or even working with them? They wear clothes from Debenhams or Adidas tops and trainers, they eat in Macdonalds and drink coffee at Starbucks, they buy CD's and read Harry Potter, they go on holiday's abroad and send emails across the world.

The deranged and cowardly murderer Jack the Ripper dissolved back into the shadows, his empty life failed even to achieve infamy because what credit could he have taken for his crimes when the criminal remained nameless. The victims, on the other hand, avenge the killer by living on through their descendants, and by them and us are remembered.

APPENDIX

In September 2007, a direct descendant of Catherine Eddowes younger sister Mary Eddowes joined the Casebook-Jack the Ripper internet site and on the message boards gave information about her connection. Apparently, the connection to Catherine had been a big family secret. I contacted the family, Roy and daughter Nadine Simmons to find out more and the following information was pieced together from their research:

After the time of the 1871 census when Mary was working at Rotherhithe in South London, she found her way north of the river and was admitted on the 14th August 1876 to the City of London Workhouse at Homerton. Her last residence was 18 Bridgewater Place in the City which suggests she could have been living with or near her sister Emma Jones. She gave her condition as single and calling as a servant.

On the 25th September 1876, Mary gave birth to an illegitimate daughter and called her Emily Eddowes when she was registered on the 29th. Both mother and daughter was discharged from the workhouse at the mother's request on the 27th November.

It seems likely that the illegitimate daughter was the reason why Mary married under the name of Elizabeth Eddowes to William Good on the 27th March 1881 at St David's Church, Upper Holloway. The witnesses was the brother and sister of the groom and therefore would not have questioned her pseudonym. Mary named her father as George Eddowes tinplate worker and lived at 40 Bride Street. Her eldest daughter Emily was put in the same school her mother had attended many years before the South Metropolitan District School at Sutton in Surrey, and it seems that Mary had told them that Emily was born in the St Olave's parish.

By the 1881 census they lived at 20 Charlton Street, Somers Town, St Pancras, where William was recorded as a coach smith. A daughter Louisa was born at Castle Road in 1883. A son William was born in 1885 when they lived in Bovingdon in Hertfordshire, Joseph was born at Bushey in 1887, George born at Rickmansworth in 1889 where they still lived in 1891 at High Street Cottages (possibly a son in between?) before Bertie was born in 1896 at Luton in Bedfordshire. Emily was back living with her mother in 1891 and married as Emily May Eddows at Luton in 1897 to Thomas William Gudgin, and had many children by him.

In 1901, the family lived at 3 Wratton Street in Hitchin, Hertfordshire. The next year Louisa Good married Ernest Bridges and had eight children one of which Doris Marie Good is the line of descent to Roy and Nadine. My thanks to Roy and Nadine for the information about Mary and her family.

Mary Ann Nichols Family Tree

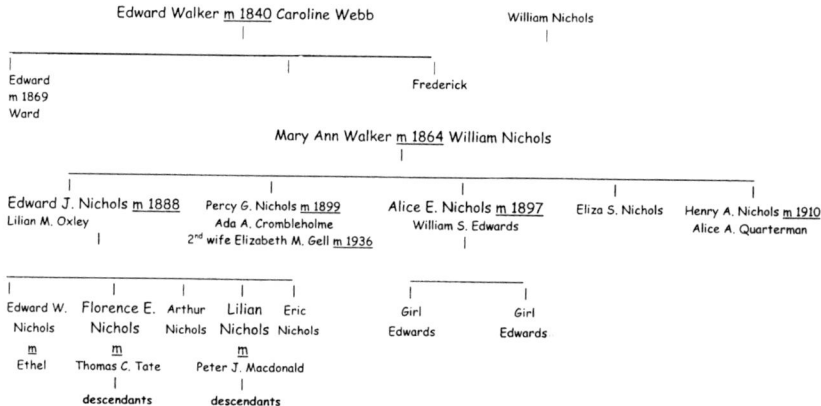

Edward Walker m 1840 Caroline Webb   William Nichols

Edward
m 1869
Ward

Frederick

Mary Ann Walker m 1864 William Nichols

Edward J. Nichols m 1888   Percy G. Nichols m 1899   Alice E. Nichols m 1897   Eliza S. Nichols   Henry A. Nichols m 1910
Lilian M. Oxley   Ada A. Crombleholme   William S. Edwards   Alice A. Quarterman
2nd wife Elizabeth M. Gell m 1936

Edward W.   Florence E.   Arthur   Lilian   Eric   Girl   Girl
Nichols   Nichols   Nichols   Nichols   Nichols   Edwards   Edwards
m   m   m
Ethel   Thomas C. Tate   Peter J. Macdonald
descendants   descendants

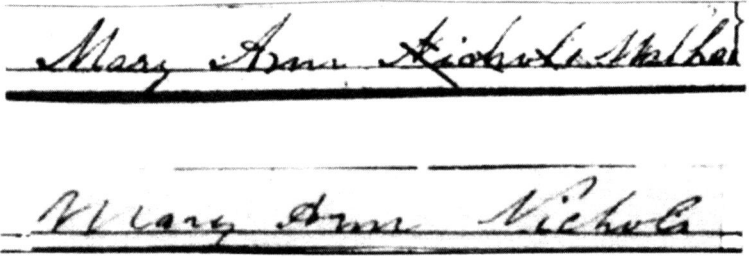

The maiden name signature of Mary Ann Nichols
and the married signature.

The grave of Mary Ann Nichols
at the City of London Cemetery.

Peabody Buildings, Lambeth, where Mary Ann Nichols
and her family lived.

Possibly Edward John Nichols, eldest son of Mary Ann Nichols.
Early 1900's?

Edward Wilfrid Nichols, eldest son of Edward John Nichols.
World War One.

Florence Elizabeth Nichols and grandson George Tate.
Florence was the eldest daughter of Edward John Nichols.

Herbert Tate, son of Florence Elizabeth Nichols. World War Two.

Dolly Tate, daughter of Florence Elizabeth Nichols,
and her nephew George Tate.

68

Lilian Nichols, daughter of Edward John Nichols.

Lilian Macdonald, daughter of Lilian Nichols, with her husband
and five children.

Maureen Adamson on her visit to Whitechapel in 2006,
standing in Osborn Street in front of the Frying Pan Public House.

Eric Nichols, son of Edward John Nichols. World War One.

Alice Esther Nichols daughter of Mary Ann Nichols, with husband
William Edwards and their two daughters. Early 1900's.

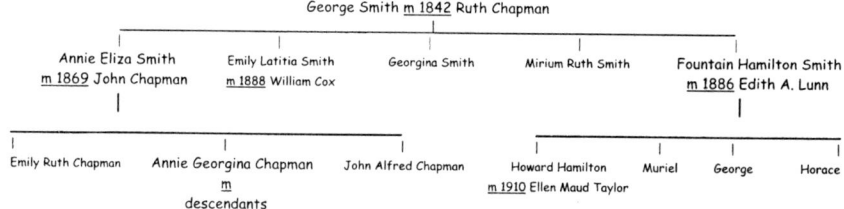

Annie Chapman Family Tree

George Smith m 1842 Ruth Chapman

| Annie Eliza Smith | Emily Latitia Smith | Georgina Smith | Mirium Ruth Smith | Fountain Hamilton Smith |
| m 1869 John Chapman | m 1888 William Cox | | | m 1886 Edith A. Lunn |

Emily Ruth Chapman	Annie Georgina Chapman	John Alfred Chapman	Howard Hamilton	Muriel	George	Horace
	m		m 1910 Ellen Maud Taylor			
	descendants					

The maiden name signature of Annie Chapman.

Newspaper illustration of Fountain Hamilton Smith,
Annie Chapman's brother.

All Saints Church, Ennismore Gardens. Annie Chapman
married there in 1869.

Annie Chapman and her husband John taken in about 1869.
The photograph has square cut corners and is stuck on a mount
which has discoloured with age.

Emily Ruth Chapman, daughter of Annie Chapman. Taken
at Brompton Photographic Studio, Wood & Co, 190 Brompton Road
no. 22610. About late 1870's.

Annie Georgina Chapman. Taken at Sutch Bros Studio,
143 Brompton Road, no 3371. About early 1880's.

Annie Georgina Chapman. Taken by F. Rich photographer of Bagshot, Surrey. When in service in the early 1890's.

Annie Georgina Chapman. Taken in her 40's.

Annie Georgina Chapman. Taken in her 70's, with her granddaughter.

St Giles-in-the-Fields Church. Elizabeth Stride married there in 1869.

Poplar and Stepney Sick Asylum. John Thomas Stride died there in 1884.

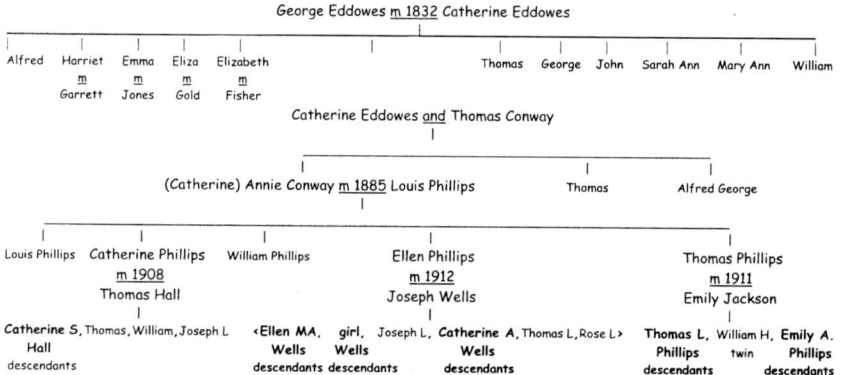

Catherine Eddowes Family Tree

George Eddowes m 1832 Catherine Eddowes

Alfred	Harriet	Emma	Eliza	Elizabeth			Thomas	George	John	Sarah Ann	Mary Ann	William
	m	m	m	m								
	Garrett	Jones	Gold	Fisher								

Catherine Eddowes and Thomas Conway

(Catherine) Annie Conway m 1885 Louis Phillips   Thomas   Alfred George

Louis Phillips	Catherine Phillips	William Phillips	Ellen Phillips					Thomas Phillips
	m 1908		m 1912					m 1911
	Thomas Hall		Joseph Wells					Emily Jackson

Catherine S, Thomas, William, Joseph L   ‹Ellen MA,   girl,   Joseph L,   Catherine A, Thomas L, Rose L›   Thomas L,   William H,   Emily A.
Hall   Wells   Wells   Phillips   twin   Phillips
descendants   descendants   descendants   descendants   descendants   descendants

ELIZA GOLD

Newspaper illustration of Eliza Gold, sister of Catherine Eddowes.

Catherine Sarah Hall, great granddaughter of Catherine Eddowes.
Taken in 1920's at Stacey's Cinema Studios, 39 Duke Street, London EC3.
Around the corner to Mitre Square.

Catherine Sarah Hall and daughter Josephine. Taken in 1940's.

Josephine, daughter of Catherine Sarah Hall.

Jan and Ian, Josephine's daughter and son.

Thomas Hall (wearing the fez), son of Catherine Phillips, with an army pal during World War Two. He was taken prisoner at Tobruk.

William Hall, son of Catherine Phillips. Taken during World War Two.

Joseph Lewis Hall, son of Catherine Phillips.

Ellen Phillips, granddaughter of Catherine Eddowes and daughter of Annie
Phillips, with husband Joseph Wells and two children, Ellen Mary Ann
Wells and Violet Wells (centre). Taken during World War One.

Ellen Mary Ann Wells with granddaughter Elizabeth. Taken in the 1980's.

Jean, daughter of Ellen Mary Ann Wells.

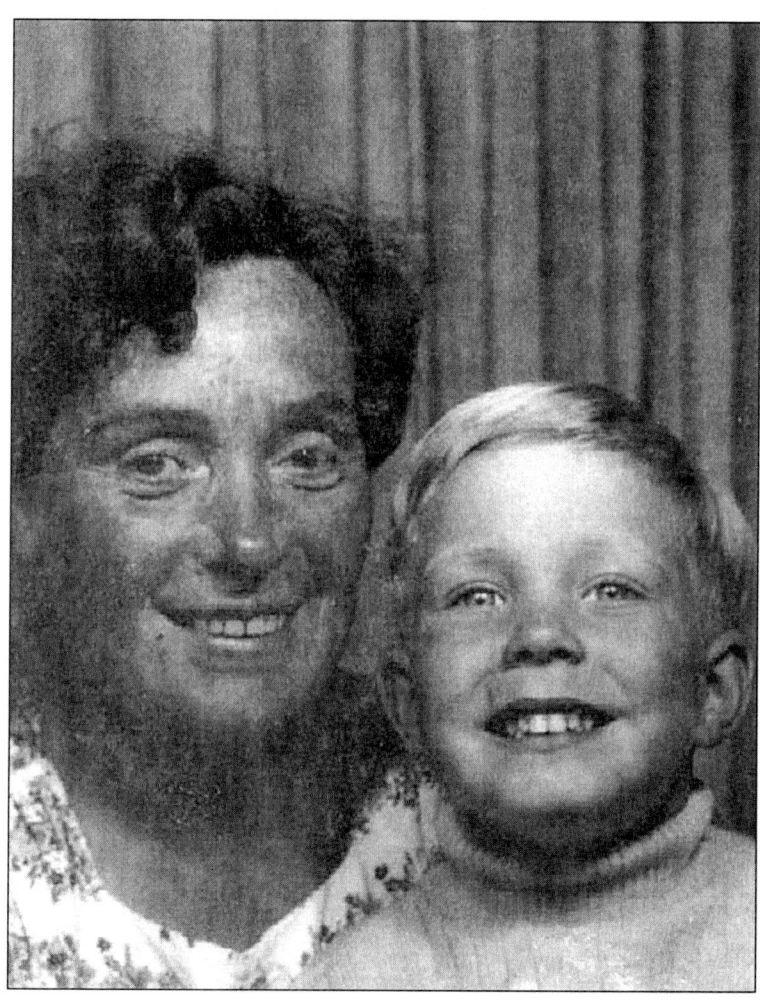

Violet Wells pictured in her 40's with son Ian.

Catherine Wells (left), daughter of Ellen Phillips, with her sister
Ellen Mary Ann.

Thomas Lewis Phillips, great grandson of Catherine Eddowes, grandson of Annie Phillips, son of Thomas Phillips. Pictured with his wife Cissy.

Emily Annie Phillips, daughter of Thomas Phillips. Pictured in 1966
with her husband and granddaughter Tracey.

Emily Annie Phillips with her great grandchildren Hayley
and Bradley (baby).

Jean Smith, daughter of Emily Annie Phillips. Taken on her wedding day
with husband George.

Thirteen direct descendants of Catherine Eddowes of all ages are pictured
in Church Passage on the walk of the 14th July 2007. The descendants
belong to the direct lines of Ellen Phillips and Thomas Phillips.

Female descendants of Catherine Eddowes on the walk standing
on the exact place where their ancestor died in 1888 at Mitre Square.

Charles William Fisher, son of Elizabeth Fisher and nephew
of Catherine Eddowes, with his wife Eliza and their child.

Printed in the United States
210387BV00004B/3/A